ASTD Trainer's WorkShop Series

Decision-Making TRAINING

Robert H. Vaughn

ASTD
PRESS
Alexandria, Virginia

ASTD Press is an internationally renowned source of insightful and practical information on workplace learning and performance topics, including training basics, evaluation and return-on-investment, instructional systems development, e-learning, leadership, and career development.

Ordering information: Books published by ASTD Press can be purchased by visiting our website at store.astd.org or by calling 800.628.2783 or 703.683.8100.

LOC: 2009923018

ISBN: 10: 1-56286-694-x
ISBN: 13: 978-1-56286-694-5

ASTD Press Editorial Staff:
Director: Dean Smith
Manager, ASTD Press: Jacqueline Edlund-Braun
Senior Associate Editor: Tora Estep
Senior Associate Editor: Justin Brusino
Editorial Assistant: Victoria Devaux
Full-Service Development and Production: Aptara Inc., Falls Church, VA, www.aptaracorp.com
    Development/Production Editors: Carol R. Field and Robin C. Bonner
    Copyeditors: Nidhi Bajaj and Carol R. Field
    Indexer: Kidd Indexing
    Proofreader: Ellen Newman
Cover Design: Ana Ilieva Foreman
Cover Illustration: Shutterstock.com

Printed by Versa Press, Inc., East Peoria, Illinois, www.versapress.com

The ASTD Trainer's WorkShop Series

◆

The ASTD Trainer's WorkShop Series is designed to be a practical hands-on road map to help you quickly develop training in key business areas. Each book in the series offers all the exercises, handouts, assessments, structured experiences, and ready-to-use presentations needed to develop effective training sessions. In addition to easy-to-use icons, each book in the series includes a companion website with PowerPoint presentations and electronic copies of all supporting material featured in the book.

Contents

◆

◆

Welcome to the start of an exciting journey—a journey not in place and time, but into the complex cognitive processes of making decisions. It's an important *human* endeavor, as well as an essential *business* skill. You have already made dozens to hundreds of decisions since you woke up this morning, so the journey is one that you've made many times. As you use this book, however, I ask that you take a fresh look, not at where you have arrived (the final decision or solution), but how you got there. It's fascinating. If you have never before taken something apart to see how it works, then you're in for a treat. I was sent to my room many times for such activities as a child, but I learned a lot.

Purpose of This Training Program

This book is designed for individuals who need to develop a training program to help others in the processes of decision making. Those activities can be quite complex, but using different kinds of "tools" can help a person approach them more easily and more effectively. In recent years, there has been a tendency for college courses and business seminars on this subject to become over-systematized. Graduate programs in management science, especially, have espoused elaborate procedures requiring an in-depth background in statistics, as well as sophisticated models into which massive amounts of data must be entered. Management science does have its place; however, most business and personal decisions simply don't require all of this.

Typical managers, entrepreneurs, and employees can make nearly all the decisions and solve most of the problems they face by just using a few simple concepts. Seldom is it necessary to deal with primary research or economic forecasting projections. Your trainees may just need to do things like figure inventory requirements or staffing needs for their department or make dozens of other routine decisions that we face on a day-to-day basis. Sophisticated models would, for these purposes, probably be inefficient and just get in the way.

This book and training program offers a "Back to Basics" training approach to decision making that is appropriate for all but upper-level managers in large organizations, and even for them at times. It will help you design a training program that can be of real, practical value on the job. Your trainees need not be experts in statistics or business theory. Some of the concepts they'll learn apply to any aspect of life; others only apply to certain kinds of business problems or decisions.

Acknowledgments

During the preparation of this Trainer's WorkShop package, I have relied significantly on two of my previous publications. The first two sections of this book include excerpts and ideas from *The Professional Trainer,* published in the second edition in 2005 by Berrett-Koehler. The decision-making ideas and presentations in section four are distilled from *Decision Making and Problem Solving in Management,* published in its third edition in 2007 by Crown Custom Publishing.

I especially appreciate the support of my colleagues and my wife, Susan, in the creation of this project. Thanks, also, to Roger Williams, a friend and former business partner who was responsible for moving both previous books into a much wider market. Mark Morrow, former acquisitions editor for ASTD Press, was quite gracious and helpful in this endeavor—as were all the ASTD staff with whom I've worked over the years. One does not create a book like this without the help of many individuals. Some of them are listed on the copyright page (page ii). Most of my direct communications were with Justin Brusino, Carol Field, and Robin Bonner, although I know many others were involved. In this age of emails, FTPs, and other distance communication, an author can be surprisingly dependent on persons he or she has never met face to face. Thanks to all of them. Finally, I particularly appreciate the constructive comments from many of my former students and seminar participants, who have helped me define the needs of their organizations to improve decision making and problem solving.

Robert H. Vaughn, PhD

Arvon Management Services

January 2010

Section One:
Introduction

◆

How to Use
This Book Effectively

- ◆ Definition of decision making

- ◆ Description of what's in this book

- ◆ Explanation of how to use this workbook most effectively

What Is Decision Making?

Everyone is required to make many decisions every day in their business and personal lives. Most decisions, by most people, are handled quickly and without much thought. But many of us procrastinate or over-analyze some of the most important decisions we must make. This book breaks down the process of making decisions into a structure that can relieve the delay and stress of choosing the right option when we face important opportunities or problems.

What's in This Book?

This book contains the materials needed to develop a professional training program on the subject of decision making. Chapters 2 through 5 help you with the training part, including how to assess the need for training, design the training, conduct the training, and evaluate whether or not your efforts were successful. Chapters 6 through 8 provide sample agendas for half-day, full-day, and two-day programs, and provide additional recommendations for putting these programs together. The remaining chapters, 9 through 18, provide the subject matter content and support needed to conduct successful training—each of these chapters is a separate module that you will use in different combinations, depending on the length of the training and the audience. These modules cover the four main content areas of the decision-making process:

- **Chapter 9:** *Module 1* is an overview of the process we all use to make decisions.

- **Chapters 10–13:** *Modules 2, 3, 4, and 5* introduce the creative, or inductive, process and tools used to come up with various options from which to make a decision.

- **Chapters 14–16:** *Modules 6, 7, and 8* cover the analytic, or deductive, process and tools used to evaluate and narrow down options to determine a final choice.

- **Chapters 17–18:** *Modules 9 and 10* detail the human and irrational aspects of decision making, as well as how a decision is accepted within an organization.

The Modules

Each of the 10 modules includes the following information:

A one- or two-sentence overview gives a brief summary of the contents, plus information provided by the module and how it fits within the structure of decision-making training.

- **Training Objectives** are two, three, or four key ideas that the participants should master as a result of the training.

- **Module Time** offers a thumbnail schedule of approximately how much time should be spent on each of the major activities in the module. All modules are either one, one and a half, or two hours in length.

- **Module Materials** lists items you should have available as you present each module, as well as some optional suggestions.

- **Module Preparation** outlines what to do before the participants arrive.

- **Sample Agenda** gives a timed list of activities referencing Power-Point slides to display and appropriate handouts and worksheets to use.

◆ **Trainer's Notes** help facilitate your training session, slide by slide. This same material is also available in the PowerPoint "Notes" section. Some step-by-step "scripting" is suggested, but use the notes included as guidelines and adapt them to your own presentation and facilitation style.

◆ **Learning Check Questions** are a collection of questions (with answers) at the end of each module that you can use as either an oral or written test. These questions are Level 2 or 3 evaluation questions (see chapter 5 for an explanation of what the levels mean). Some discussion questions are "short answer," whereas others are multiple choice. You will also find suggested handouts and worksheets already assigned for the class.

◆ **PowerPoint Slides** (11 to 23) are included with each module. The slides are shown as thumbnails at the end of each module and are available as downloads from the web at www.astd.org/decision-makingtraining. The slides are designed to be easily customizable and do not include PowerPoint features such as transitions, sounds, or other complicating factors. Make whatever changes are appropriate and add any backgrounds, company logos, sounds, transitions, style changes, and so on, that meet your needs. Also remember that not all computers and projectors will treat the files the same way, so you should definitely test the slides on the equipment you will actually be using. If the company or room in which you are doing training does not have PowerPoint capability, the slides can be printed and copied as transparencies for use on an overhead projector.

◆ **Worksheets** are part of the training, with one to six included with each module.

◆ **Evaluations Instruments,** one standard form for modules and one for the full program, are provided at the end of chapter 5.

See "Online Materials," below. All of the PowerPoint slides, worksheets, and evaluations are available for download at www.astd.org/decisionmakingtraining.

How to Use This Workbook

This book covers the process of decision making. If you have not done organizational training before, you will find lots of helpful suggestions and references to make your initial effort easier and more professional. If you have done training before, you will probably want to skim through this part for both refreshers and new ideas as you approach the design of this program.

The module design of this book offers the trainer maximum flexibility to create the right training for the intended audience and time available. The suggested combinations are model programs, but the modules can be used individually or in any combination to meet your training needs.

Those familiar with our *WorkShop* books will notice that this format is a bit different from other titles in the series. The handouts and worksheets appear at the end of the chapter or module in which they are used, rather than together in a separate chapter.

Online Materials

The module training materials—including PowerPoint slides, worksheets, and evaluations—can be accessed at www.astd.org/decisionmakingtraining. All the materials can be easily downloaded and printed from this website. Follow the instructions in the Appendix, "Using the Online Materials," at the back of this workbook.

Icons

Clock indicates recommended timeframes for specific activities

Worksheet indicates worksheets or handouts that you can print or copy to support training activities.

Assessment appears when an agenda or learning activity includes an assessment.

PowerPoint Slide indicates PowerPoint presentations and slides that can be used individually.

Exercise introduces participant exercises.

What to Do Next highlights actions that will help you make the transition from one section of this workbook to the next, or from one training activity to another within a training module.

Learning Check Questions points out questions you can use to explore significant aspects of the training.

What to Do Next

- ◆ Study the contents of this workbook to familiarize yourself with the material it offers.

- ◆ Download the online content and review the files so that you understand how the material is organized.

Section Two:
Training Basics

◆

Assessing the Needs of Participants

- ◆ A discussion of typical learners and how to uncover specific training needs

- ◆ How to ensure that the training is the right answer to the participants' needs

- ◆ How to conduct a simple needs analysis

"Never try to teach a pig to sing. It wastes your time and annoys the pig." That anonymous piece of wisdom comes from a sign my uncle has hanging on the porch of his bed-and-breakfast in Emigrant, Montana. You shouldn't try to teach people something they don't need to know. Find out first exactly what your participants need.

Who Are Your Typical Learners?

Everybody makes decisions, and the book you are now reading may, of course, be purchased by a variety of different organizations and independent trainers. Indeed, some aspects of decision-making training can benefit nearly anyone. But as a good trainer, you should know your audience and design the training around each class of participants.

Authors Kenneth W. Houp and Thomas E. Pearsall have suggested one method of classifying the audience in their book *Reporting Technical Information:*

Experts: People who have advanced degrees or at least several years of formal practice in a subject.

Technicians: People who know the nuts and bolts of a topic but perhaps not the theories behind it or the nuances involved. They could repair the machine, but not build it from scratch.

Executives: People who mainly have an interest in a subject, but who may not care about its actual working processes.

Laypersons: People who have only a passing knowledge and interest in the subject.

Mixed or Unknown Audiences: Just what the name implies.

Experts love facts, will challenge assumptions, and need to be convinced on a theoretical level. They are a very demanding audience. This book is not going to be useful for training people who are already experts in decision making.

Although a person may be expert in other areas, he or she may qualify only as a layperson in the subject of decision making. This book will be useful for training people who are experts in their own fields but need to know more about decision making.

The technician wants to know the mechanics and process of the topic. Technicians who make decisions will probably appreciate the structure that this training program provides in module 1 and further on. They will want to break the process apart and study each piece to make it better, and that is what this program will help them do.

The executive will look at making decisions from a management or cost-benefit or "value" perspective. In fact, executives may be your most eager audience. They will want to apply the concepts to their day-to-day jobs.

The layperson will be interested in the big picture, but will rely on the training for details and information at a more basic (rather than technical) level. Laypeople will respond to practical and personal anecdotal examples, such as deciding which car or house to buy. The exercises in this book will help personalize the training for them.

The combined or unknown audience can best be addressed by compartmentalizing the training. This way, information of interest to each learner can be extracted without requiring complete review and understanding of the whole package. This may mean that certain people will opt out of some module sessions, or that you may need to be flexible about how the material is presented, or that discussions need to be divided into subgroups of participants who have the same goals in common.

That's why, to better understand your audience, you should perform some type of needs analysis.

The sources of data for this analysis will include (1) key individuals within (and sometimes outside) the organization, (2) job descriptions, (3) quantitative data such as costs, sales projections, or staffing requirements, and (4) any information about impending changes that will require participants to acquire new skills and knowledge.

Needs Analysis: Why Is Decision-Making Training Taking Place?

Why was it decided to offer this training? There must have been some reason—perhaps a few bad decisions were made and an executive decided that training was needed to remedy the situation. Whatever the reason, you need to know at least a little bit about who will be in the training program and what they are expected to get out of it.

Trainers don't always get the opportunity to perform a needs analysis before they begin a training program. If the request for decision-making training came from a formal study, the proposal may offer useful information about why this training was suggested. Most of the time, however, requests for training come when someone with the authority suggests it: "Why don't we have a training program in decision making?" As a result, you are now going through this book trying to figure out how to help make it happen.

If you find yourself with the opportunity to do a formal needs analysis, you should review one or more of the training books suggested in the "For Further Reading" section at the end of this book and choose a process that meets your needs and level of comfort. You'll need to define how your participants should be making decisions, determine their current skills, and understand the difference between their expected and actual performance. From that analysis, you will be able to develop specific training objectives and choose which parts of this program will help to narrow the difference between expected and actual behaviors. It is beyond the scope of this book to provide the resources and specifics necessary to conduct a formal needs analysis, but we will look at some methods to use to conduct an informal analysis.

HOW CAN I PERFORM A SIMPLE NEEDS ANALYSIS?

Because a complete, formal needs analysis process is not going to be an option for many of you, here are some practical and expedient ways to find out about your participants before you walk into the classroom. These methods can be used individually or in combination, and they are listed in order from the most time consuming to something that can be done in just a few minutes. Whatever you do, it will be to your benefit as the trainer to know something about your participants and the nature of their jobs before you design or present a training program to them.

Observation. Spend time with a few of the identified participants in their work environment while you are designing the program. Find out what sort of decisions they are required to make on the job and how they currently make them.

Records, Reports, or Work Samples. Search through the organization's records or reports that may help you understand the nature of decisions in these people's jobs and how they make them.

Key Consultation. Meet with some key individuals to discuss how decisions are made in the organization. Key individuals might include the future participants, their supervisors, co-workers, perhaps even customers and others who understand the jobs the participants are supposed to be doing.

Group Discussion. Get a group of the key people together to help you plan the program. Talk about issues or concerns they have regarding how decision making is done in their jobs and what training they would like to see for themselves and other prospective participants. People often find it difficult to dissect the decision-making process they use, so be sure to have some questions prepared to lead the discussion.

Survey. Use the survey questionnaire provided (Worksheet 2–1) at the end of this chapter and in the support materials for this book, or design your own survey instrument to obtain insight regarding the participants' jobs and the organizational environment as they relate to decision making. The survey is useful in several ways; however, it is weak in that it describes the responders' impressions of themselves rather than the more objective and evidence-based techniques mentioned earlier (that show you how they are seen by *others*). But it is far better to use a survey than to do *no* preliminary analysis at all, and using one will prompt the participants' thinking on the subject. A survey can even be done at the start of the training, although doing it that late won't help you with the design process.

What If We Can't Do a Participant Assessment?

Trainers often walk into the training session not knowing for sure what objectives should be met or what skills the participants have. In that case, seasoned trainers reach into their bag of tricks to dazzle participants with showmanship. There is no substitute for experience and a repertoire of standby techniques, tricks, worksheet forms, and interactive questions.

For example, in a situation where the participants' needs or skill levels are unclear, you might start the training program using a deductive mode—that is, the trainer guides the learner to an understanding by posing situations and asking questions of the learner—to quickly get a feel for where the participants are. The trainer who instead starts inductively—rambling on for hours without realizing the presentation is over the participants' heads—risks boring the audience to tears. So come to class prepared to be flexible with the training. Apply the principles of adult learning discussed in this chapter, and let the participants help you. Begin by doing an in-class needs analysis: Deconstruct the job using a flipchart to collect and evaluate the groups' needs and expectations. A tool such as the needs analysis questionnaire (see below) can also help you get a quick feel for the group.

Using the Needs Analysis Questionnaire

Worksheet 2–1 can be used to prepare a needs analysis prior to or at the start of a decision-making skills training program. (If you have not already reviewed this worksheet, which can be found at the end of this chapter, take a moment to look over it.) Participants should be directed to make a mark somewhere between the extremes on each line to indicate *how they assess their current mode of operation*, as a decision maker on the job. They should not spend a lot of time mulling over their responses. Limit them to no more than five minutes. Encourage participants to be honest in their responses. Assure them that their responses will be kept anonymous and that their answers cannot be right or wrong.

To tally the results, make a transparency of the form and place it over the top of each of the individual forms in turn, making a mark on top of each of the participants' marks. (You could also remove the dashed line and use a mathematical rating such as 1–10 for each item; however, that way you lose much of the data a visual representation can provide.)

It's likely that many participants will agree on some topics, shown by a clustering of the marks in one area, and many will disagree on others, where the marks range from one end of the scale to the other. If this analysis is done before or early on in a training program, such information can help you plan or adjust the emphasis of the training (more below). The resulting summary can be shared with the participants. It will help show the diversity or agreement of approaches indicated by their classmates.

Advantage: This type of questionnaire is quick to design and easy to complete and compile the results. You can add additional questions or delete or reword questions in the document. The questionnaire can give you both specific information about the participants and an indication of their attitudes and beliefs.

Disadvantage: The responses represent the participants' *opinions only*; therefore, the results may not be accurate. A questionnaire is certainly not a substitute for a thorough needs analysis, but it can be a useful fallback tool or a good opening activity for the training.

HOW CAN ANSWERS TO THE QUESTIONNAIRE INFLUENCE THE PROGRAM DESIGN?

First, look for clusters of commonality in the results. For example, if most of the respondents to item 2 make their marks on the right side of the line (indicating they make decisions only after much study and thought), it might be good to emphasize some of the points in module 9, such as that thinking too much often leads to poorer-quality decisions than just going with your gut.

Next, look for response patterns that are very diverse, where marks range widely from left to right. The lesson for you and the participants is that everyone is different, and that what one person disagrees with or finds boring in class may be new and exciting information to another person. This insight can be used to heighten awareness for the group.

Finally, look for a pattern where two distinct subgroups seem to emerge, with a cluster of marks to the left for one group and to the right end of the line for another group. In that case, you might choose to exploit these identified differences to encourage debate or to create working groups within the class.

Once you have looked for the patterns, consider what general information can be gleaned from the specific questions. For example, items 12 and 15 may guide your approach to running the class. If a majority of people prefer to listen and take notes, you might choose to increase the amount of time you use simply presenting ideas versus discussing or debating ideas during the training. (Of course, as you will read in the next chapter, this may not be the best way to train adults, even though they might prefer to be passive in learning.)

WORKSHEET ITEMS AND THEIR SIGNIFICANCE TO DECISION MAKING

See Worksheet 2–1, on page 19, before reviewing the following items.

Item 1. Usually people who want to decide things for themselves (left side) are more creative. People who tend to the right side usually like this training program.

Item 2. Some decisions do need careful thought, but most decisions we make tend to suffer from too much analysis. Good discussion question: Which decisions should be made quickly?

Item 3. Easygoing people tend to be able to relax more and may be more creative. They may also be disorganized or not focus on efficiency or organizational goals as well as others do,

Item 4. Stressed people (right side) often spend too much time procrastinating and being indecisive. Improving their decision-making process may help them relax a little more.

Item 5. Some decisions profit from group input; other decisions are better made individually. The range of responses to this question may also influence how much group work you include in the training design.

Item 6. Responses on both sides need not change the training design. If people on the right side tend to not be creative, modules 2 through 5 may help them to improve.

Item 7. Some things need to be in writing, some things shouldn't be. Discussion question: When should you use each of the methods?

Item 8. Unlike item 5, this question asks about day-to-day activities instead of work on a particular project.

Item 9. Your analysis of the responses to this question may determine how much time you spend on modules 6 through 8, especially module 7, or whether you even want to cover it at all.

Item 10. Remember that we're dealing with perceptions here. All responses are "correct," although each response may be influenced by that person's own attitudes.

Item 11. The responses here may influence how much time you spend on module 9, and also tell you how easily participants will deal with the deductive material in modules 6 through 8.

Item 12. Responses here will help you design the training program—and help you anticipate how the end-of-training evaluations will come out.

Item 13. Participants who have had lots of training about management techniques may already be aware of many of the tools to be covered, and perhaps should not go through it all again.

Item 14. Experience helps, and people who have made a great number of organizational decisions may be able to give you great examples in discussion sessions.

Item 15. Compare with responses to item 12, but don't use the responses as an excuse to lecture exclusively throughout the program.

What to Do Next

- ◆ Determine who needs to be involved in the analysis, including training participants and any stakeholders.

- ◆ Decide the most effective needs analysis methods to use to gather pertinent data from your participants.

Worksheet 2–1

Decision Making: Needs Analysis

Instructions: Place a mark anywhere on the dotted line in relation to the statement that best describes you.

1. I am more comfortable if I am given

An end goal only .... Details and an exact process

2. I tend to make decisions

Quickly, then act
on them .... After much study and thought

3. On the job, I am personally

Easygoing and
relaxed .... Constantly focused on work

4. I personally use my time at work so that I

Get everything
done easily .... Am often behind in work

5. I am most comfortable working on a project

By myself .... With a group

6. I believe that I am

Creative; I see
the big picture .... Excellent at working details

7. I would rather communicate with people by

Talking with
them .... Sending them memos or emails

8. In my current position, I deal more often with

Individuals .... Work groups

9. My comfort level with numerical information is

Very high; I deal
easily with it .... I can do math, but really don't like to

10. Most of my co-workers will usually

Do a good job .... Goof off if they can

11. My co-workers would describe me as

Driven by my
emotions .... An analytical and logical person

12. I would personally prefer to get from a decision-making program

Background, for
use on my own .... Direct, specific suggestions

13. I have had formal training in management or supervision

None, to very little
at all .... A college degree or the equivalent

14. I have had experience in making organizational decisions

None, or only at
a very low level .... Major financial decisions

15. In a training program, I prefer to

Listen and take
notes .... Discuss and challenge ideas

© 2010 *Decision-Making Training*, American Society for Training & Development

◆

Designing Interactive Training

What's in This Chapter?

- ◆ An explanation of adult learning principles

- ◆ The difference between deductive and inductive learning

- ◆ How to use the sample designs in the book

- ◆ Tips on designing effective training

How Do Adults Learn?

Perhaps the best way to understand adult learning is to think about your own learning experiences. Most people have been taught in a predictable fashion during childhood. The adults (teachers) had the knowledge, and the children (learners) didn't. The authority figure "dispensed" the knowledge. Children learn because they trust the authority figures who say they need to learn what is being taught, or sometimes even because the children really want to learn it. Children also trust that the teachers know what they are talking about. When you were young and naïve (an "open book"), such a learning style was necessary and maybe appropriate. Adults, however, come to a training program under very different circumstances.

Adults need to be able to put new learning into a context or frame of reference based on their existing knowledge.

A major difference between the way children and adults learn is explained by what each brings to the learning situation (Table 3–1). Adults usually bring a better understanding of *why* they need to learn certain skills and facts. They also bring more background experiences than children, and may already have formed an opinion about what is being taught. Adults are more often used to being in charge; they dislike the lack of control they experience in a typical classroom. Trainers who use the same approach for adults as they would for children will miss the adults' quite different outlook and needs.

Table 3–1

Differences Between Child and Adult Learning

CHARACTERISTIC	CHILDREN	ADULTS
Method of operating in general	◆ Are dependent and varied, with few common experiences ◆ Don't know their own needs and are not asked ◆ Have trouble relating learning to real world ◆ Are often unable to understand relevance because of limited experiences ◆ Are often willing to try and fail.	◆ Are independent, yet have many common experiences ◆ Are capable of self-direction ◆ Have a high need for relevance, and will ask: "What's in it for me?" and expect a good answer ◆ Seek out training to cope with life-change events ◆ Seek accuracy; avoid trial and error.
Method of operating during learning	◆ Have a high dependence on teacher ◆ See the relationship with the trainer as a child-to-parent relationship ◆ Need the teacher to develop curriculum ◆ Learn mostly for future use.	◆ Learn from each other as well as trainer ◆ See the relationship with the trainer as an adult-to-adult relationship ◆ May need help defining their needs ◆ Learn for immediate needs as well as future use ◆ May need time to unlearn ideas and challenge current beliefs.
Implications for the teacher or trainer	◆ Teacher will take role of expert—giver of information ◆ Teachers need illustrations that will be understood by all, or most, of the class ◆ Trainers must give frequent examples to learners ◆ Students may not have common background experiences to build on ◆ Students often enjoy "survey" courses (i.e., a superficial overview of topics).	◆ Trainer will take the role of catalyst—arranger of experiences, mediator, facilitator, processor, and occasionally expert ◆ Trainers need to draw on their experiences and use them to illustrate points ◆ Trainees will learn from use of analogies, similes, and so on ◆ Trainees often avoid survey courses; they prefer to focus on specific problems and issues.

© Robert H. Vaughn

Inductive vs. Deductive Learning

Part of the difference in training for children and adults has to do with how the trainer uses *inductive* or *deductive* approaches.

With the inductive style, the trainer tells the learner what needs to be known. Delivering a lecture is typical of the inductive style.

The deductive style is also known as the "Socratic method," named after Socrates, the philosopher and teacher who rarely told his students anything, but instead asked questions of them. Some also call it the "aha!" style of training, in which the trainer guides the learner to an understanding by posing situations and asking questions of the learner. The learners then synthesize previously known facts into a higher level of knowledge. Case studies are an example of a deductive style of teaching and learning. Most training programs incorporate a combination of inductive and deductive styles, although not always in the right proportions.

Children are frequently taught using the inductive style because of their limited experience with a particular topic, as well as with life in general. Adults, on the other hand, will only occasionally need an entirely inductive style of training. Adults may need to be trained inductively if the subject matter is (1) completely new to them, (2) unstructured or illogical, or (3) physically dangerous. The inductive style may also be best where physical damage or loss of productivity could occur as a result of the training. For example, we want to tell a participant not to wear loose clothing around a rotating machine, rather than let them find out from experience. In those situations, adults should be told the facts and the rules for dealing with them, and not left to discover facts or procedures for themselves. Most of the time, however, the deductive approach will work better for adults for a variety of reasons, not the least of which is that it *involves* them in the learning process. Adults learn best as active learners working on simulations or problems that they perceive to be relevant to the workplace.

Adults need to feel respected, and they may think inductive training "talks down to" them. The deductive approach to training also helps participants learn the concepts behind the facts and procedures instead of just the facts and procedures themselves. This helps them integrate new information with old, instead of trying to just add on more data. Table 3–2 suggests situations in which each of the two styles is appropriate for adult training.

Table 3–2
Inductive Versus Deductive Training for Adults

VARIABLE	USE INDUCTIVE WHEN	USE DEDUCTIVE WHEN
Participants' entering behavior	Learner has no (or very limited) relevant knowledge of the subject	Learner knows the facts or has experience in related areas
Nature of subject	Subject can be learned step-by-step, rather than intuitively Physical safety or cost concerns rule out a deductive approach	Subject matter permits a variety of means to an end and a logical, intuitive structure
Trainer's ability	The trainer has a limited grasp of subject or not much teaching experience	Trainer knows subject and thus can deal with interactive dynamics
Time limitations	Circumstances dictate covering lots of subject matter in a little time Preparation time is limited.	Adequate time is available for the training Adequate preparation is possible.

Do All Adults Learn in The Same Way?

Tables 3–1 and 3–2 highlight the differences between adults and children. But the classifications of "adults" and "children" are rather broad and subjective. Not all adult learners are the same. Humans, irrespective of age, vary from person to person and topic to topic in how they learn best. A number of models exist to describe how individual adults prefer to learn. In the past decade, research has improved our understanding of "learning styles."

How Should I Use the Sample Designs in This Book?

Although this book has been developed to help the novice trainer and to provide lots of information on the subject of decision making, you will not be able to walk into the first class without preparation. In the previous chapter, we discussed how to assess the needs of the learners. Now, you must design a plan to meet those needs. Later, chapters 6, 7, and 8 will guide you through the various training designs that this book supports.

The most important thing at this point is to determine which parts of the training you will need to provide for the learners, get familiar with that material, and then use the suggested designs to create a training plan.

Why Is a Training Plan Important?

A trainer can't show up at the appointed time and ask, "What shall we talk about today?" any more than a supervisor could show up in an office or on the shop floor and say, "What shall we make today?" Both need to plan. Both need to control and give feedback. Your training plan should

- ensure the training objectives are met

- keep training on schedule and on budget

- provide a reference for the trainer during the instruction ("notes")

- document the training for organization

- enable multiple trainers to teach the same program.

As you develop your training plan, keep in mind that you want to make it as practical and viable for your learners as you can.

How Can I Make the Learning Experience Attractive to Adults?

A number of options make training more palatable for adults. Effective training is, of course, actually a lot more complicated than just following a checklist. But for now, here are some ideas that work well for training adults:

Set Positive Expectations. Keep training as risk free as possible. Many adults have been negatively conditioned by poor training experiences in the past. They frequently approach training sessions with those old concerns in mind. Adults don't want to look foolish to their peers, so the trainer should do whatever is reasonable to establish the experience as positive and non-threatening. The trainer creates the environment, but the participants can help develop positive expectations for the learning experience.

Use Appropriate Motivations and Rewards. Reduce ambivalence to learning. Most learning isn't something that happens automatically or unconsciously. It's an activity that we decide to do or not do. Knowing that, the trainer needs to clearly spell out the benefits to learning. Motivation can be positive or negative, of course. One can motivate by saying, "Learn to do this and you will enjoy your job more, get a raise, and be able to retire happy and fulfilled." Or, one can motivate by saying, "Learn to do this by next week, or you're fired." Positive motivation is usually preferable, but negative motivation may also work (but expect consequences). It depends in large part on the individual participants.

Allow for Unlearning Time, If Necessary. Sometimes adults bring excess baggage to the training. Keep in mind that some people show up with good ideas and experience, others arrive with poor ideas or experience that don't match the situation, and still others bring no relevant ideas or experience at all. When participants show up with incorrect ideas or old ways of doing things—for example, inefficient methods for doing a task—then extra time and clear reasons to *unlearn* must be given before the participants can tune themselves into learning a more efficient method for doing the task.

Make the Training Relevant. Adults want specific, practical, and life-like situations that will satisfy their needs and interests. Adults want to see immediate benefits from the material they're learning. Explain why they need to learn what is being taught. Give them concrete examples of how the training will benefit them on the job. This will be easier if you follow the processes outlined in the next chapter, and if you can work with the supervisors of the participants before, during, and after the training sessions.

Use the Concept of "Just-In-Time" Training. Training that can be immediately applied provides additional motivation and a sense of urgency. Whenever possible, initiate technical training before using that new skill in the workplace, allowing enough time for assimilation and practice before the knowledge is used on the job.

Sequence the Training Appropriately. A popular book in the training field is *Telling Ain't Training*. The title says it all—simply presenting a collection of relevant information to participants does not qualify as training. The data must be organized in some logical, cohesive fashion using principles of instructional design. Frequently, presenters will offer ideas beginning with the easiest or most basic and moving to the difficult or most complex. But some training may be better presented by working from the first step to the last or from known to unknown. The sequence should also allow for variations in the pace and intensity of the training. Malcolm Knowles, a pioneer in adult education, points out the difference between a content plan and a process design. The latter is much more difficult. Further suggestions on the subjects of sequencing, pacing, and other lesson design ideas are to be found in chapter 4, which covers conducting the training.

Recognize That Adults Have Short Attention Spans. Many researchers claim that adults have even shorter attention spans than children. Training works best when offered in "bite-sized chunks." A chunk is a key piece of information, a module, a natural unit of work, or some logical subdivision of the whole to be learned.

Involve the Learners. Learning is more rapid and efficient when the learner is a participant, rather than a spectator. Learning based on the learner's past experience will be easier to grasp and better retained.

Have the Learners Do Something or Create Something. Learning must be used for it to be retained. It should be applied immediately. A visible and tangible product as a result of the learning stimulates interest and accelerates learning. It also supports participants who prefer a kinesthetic learning style.

Speak Their Language. Participants want to feel that the trainer understands their situation. When they hear the trainer frequently speak in the abstract or use too many "textbook terms," they will be put off, and may question the trainer's credibility. Trainers should be familiar with the industry and jargon of the participants' workplace.

Use Appropriate Training Techniques and Support. It would be a very poor training technique to give a lecture about art or music without also using some visuals or sound. The chosen training techniques must match the topic. Art is a visual medium, thus it should usually be taught visually. Music is an aural medium; it requires sound to support effective understanding by the participants. Another reason to use various techniques is to engage more of the senses. Learners remember what they see longer than what they hear, and what they do even longer than what they see. Using problem-solving methods and materials heightens interest and learning. How to apply appropriate training techniques will be covered in later chapters.

Ask Questions. Questions help you find out how the participants are doing, and questioning involves them in the process much more actively. But obvious questions such as "Are there any questions?" or "Do you understand?" don't go far enough. Questions should push participants to respond to what they have just learned. This is an important distinction.

Promote Concentration. Control the physical learning environment to help the participants focus on the task at hand. This includes such things as requiring that cell phones be turned off, and minimizing distractions such as activity outside the windows or noise in the room. Vary the stimuli and pacing of the content and activities, and otherwise do what you can to help the participants focus. Hold the training off site, if possible, or limit the distractions and interruptions if the training is held on site. Also, be sure to provide occasional breaks to ensure participants don't lose their concentration.

Tap Into Group Dynamics. A number of people working together with common interests learn faster than the same persons working alone. Adults don't always need the input or feedback of a trainer—they can learn from peers. The trainer's role may be simply to ensure that the learning occurs and is accurate. Besides, participants will often work in teams when they get back to the job, and encouraging this during training may have the added benefit of building bonds and interpersonal skills.

Where Do I Begin?

Designing an effective training plan will take some time to do properly. You will need to think through your training strategies. Worksheet 3–1 is a good place to begin.

Answers to many of the questions (the objectives, for example) can be taken right out of your audience needs analysis and from the pages of this book.

What to Do Next

- ◆ Review your training plan and the suggestions discussed in this chapter.

- ◆ Make some detailed notes in the training plan where you expect to use specific ideas from this chapter.

- ◆ Design your training plan.

Worksheet 3–1
Preplanning for Training Program

Instructions: Use this worksheet to prepare for your upcoming training program. Use additional sheets as necessary.

Name of Trainer _____ Date _____

Training Program _____

Training Design Issues

The title of the job-related training session you will conduct

_____

This training is needed because

_____

The person (or department) who requested this training is

_____

The participants are expected to have this level of knowledge or skill base when they begin

_____

The key objective(s) of the training is (are)

_____

_____

The benefits to the participants if they learn and apply the training include

_____

_____

The main points that will be covered are

_____

Information that needs to be visualized (by demonstration or audio-visual) or practiced (hands-on exercises) includes

_____

Points that need to be made in a conclusion of the training include

_____

The participants' manager is expecting the following to happen as a result of this training

_____

continued on next page

Worksheet 3–1, continued
Preplanning for Training Program

This group of participants was chosen because

_____

If a similar or related training program was previously conducted, the result was

_____

The following offices and individuals can help in preparing for this training

_____

The level of success of the program will be determined by

_____

Training Logistics Issues

The date(s), starting and ending times for the training will be

_____

The location for the training program is

_____

The number and types of participants in the training session will include

_____

The attendees will be informed about the training how, when, and by whom?

_____

Equipment (supplies, materials, samples, handouts, visuals and other items) that will be needed includes

_____

Deadline dates

Obtaining information   _____
Organizing outline   _____
Preparing visuals   _____
Practicing   _____
Previewing for management   _____
Finalizing   _____
Evaluating   _____

Other significant items to consider include

_____

© 2004 Robert H. Vaughn

Conducting the Training

- Where to begin and how training sessions are normally conducted

- Comparison of academic and training models

- Tips on how to engage learners and encourage participation, and the role of the facilitator

- Methods for using subgroups in training and wrapping up a session

Where Should I Start?

Delivering successful training begins by planning to succeed. Here is list of considerations, trainer characteristics, and goals you should try to achieve in your training.

Get Everything Ready Ahead of Time

Make proper arrangements at the training location. Notify participants and their supervisors of the training's location, time, and other requirements. Arrange for refreshments or lunch, if appropriate. Prepare enough handouts and training materials for each participant. Distribute name tags or name tents (placards). Gather all your supplies and equipment, including your training plan, videos, flipchart, markers, business cards, and so on. Decide if you want to use music at the beginning of class as people enter or during breaks. Prepare the room by adjusting the seating and making sure the lighting and temperature are comfortable.

Make a Good First Impression

Dress appropriately for the training you'll be giving; you don't want to be significantly overdressed or more casual than the participants.

Be in the training area before the participants arrive, and greet them as they arrive. Materials should be laid out for the participants; the furniture arranged as you want it; and media equipment in place, booted up, and focused correctly on the screen.

If you choose to use an icebreaker of any sort, make sure it's both relevant and appropriate to the audience. Keep in mind that if it's a short program, the icebreaker also needs to be short, or omitted entirely.

Start on time. That sets a good example: It shows that you take the training seriously and expect participants to, as well.

At the very start, deal with any housekeeping issues, such as letting people know a general schedule (including when breaks will probably happen), where the restrooms are located, any rules on interruptions (cell phones, knocks at the door), any rules on food and drink in the training room, and so on.

Establish Your Credibility Early

Participants need to know why you are the trainer and to feel confident that they can learn something from you. In business training, it is seldom enough just to have academic credentials. Participants want to hear what you've done that relates to the training. It's even better if you've done it in their company or at least know about their company.

Of course, now and then, trainers are put into situations where they are required to train on something they don't know all that well. If you find yourself in this situation, here are a couple of suggestions. Explain why you have been designated as the trainer. Maybe it's because you are their supervisor or have some position of authority in the organization. Maybe it's because you have some special knowledge of the topic, even if you don't have experience. Go around the class and ask what experience the participants bring. If their experience is more than yours, point out how much they can add to the program and emphasize your role as a facilitator rather than as a subject-matter expert. Also, you might begin with relevant stories from inside or outside the organization, which will get participants involved in the subject and indicate that you have planned effectively to cover the topic.

Above all, do not exaggerate your experience, but also never undermine your credibility by drawing attention to your inexperience. If you are asked questions you can't answer, tell the participants that you'll get back to them, and then do it. Exaggerating your experience or guessing at an answer will undercut your credibility quickly, and, once lost, credibility can't be regained. If you have planned an effective lesson, you should have the confidence to carry it off well.

Determine the Motivations of Your Participants

People come to training programs for a variety of reasons. Some volunteer to come, whereas others are directed to come. Some are excited about learning new things, whereas others are concerned about keeping their jobs. Some merely will be filling a seat or attending only because they must. Although it's not good to let those people off the hook too easily, you should be wary of letting them drag down the rest of the group or letting them sap too much of your energy. If everyone else "gets into" the training, they may come along; if not, just accept that you can't force a horse to drink (or a learner to think).

Use Your Students' Backgrounds

As you learn the strengths and weaknesses of individual participants, you can structure the learning experience for them, either with or without their help. First, determine if the group is homogeneous or heterogeneous in terms of levels of experience with the subject matter.

Groups that are either "all experienced" or "all *in*experienced" can be easier to deal with from a training plan point of view, because they all need the same information. But a mixed group can also provide benefits for the trainer—for example, using the skills and experience of the participants to help teach the less experienced. This has two advantages: Adult students learn better when they teach others, and the novices gain the benefit of their classmates' experience.

If the group consists of all novices, the trainer will have to rely more on his or her personal experiences, plus any case studies, readings, exercises, and other materials selected to help bring the points home. Obviously, course topics such as decision making can be related to many things, which even novices have experienced.

If the participants are all "old hands" at the subject, it is important to guard against the "I-know-it-all" syndrome. This may be particularly true if you are seen as either a "peer" or as an "academic" who has not been on the firing line. Sometimes a pretest can raise awareness, by helping learners recognize the gaps in their understanding. You may also need to point out that changes in the workplace require that everyone needs to keep current, even if he or she performs his or her current job very well. The fact is, bad habits creep into everyone's work, and training is one way to help get back on track.

Mixed groups of learners present the biggest challenge to handle. Recruiting the more skilled to help train the less skilled is one option. This can be done by creating mixed teams of skilled and unskilled learners. Another technique is to vary the training style with a range of exercises so that even the experienced students are actively engaged. Sometimes it is possible to modularize the training and allow more skilled people to skip portions they already have mastered.

Treat Learners Like Adults

Adults often come into a class feeling they should know it all already. They may be defensive and reluctant to admit their weaknesses. They need to see a clear purpose and application for the training—it has to be practical. Be sure to tie in examples with their own experiences. Talk *with* them, not *at* them. Even subject-matter experts can contribute in the classroom, and they often prefer to participate rather than just listen to a lecture.

What Is the Typical Flow of a Training Session?

Most training sessions comprise one or more cycles and will go through a predictable sequence of activities. The following stages are common in effective training plans and may be repeated as needed:

1. *Introduction.* Start the training session with something that will either capture the attention of the participants or motivate and interest them. Your opener should create anticipation about the training with a display of visual aids, outlines, artifacts, and so on.

2. *Objectives.* Let the participants know where they are headed. Learners benefit from a mental framework to help them structure their learning of new information. Outline what will be covered, how they will use it, and how they will be evaluated.

3. *Information.* This is the content of the lesson. It should follow the statement of objectives and comprise clearly defined parts. Use a variety of inductive and deductive methods in the presentation. Accommodate different learning styles. Tell, show, illustrate, and ask questions of the participants to help them develop the knowledge or skill being taught and to make certain they understand.

4. *Demonstrations.* If an objective is for people to learn a *skill*, break the content down into discrete steps and present them in the correct order. Demonstrate what a person who has the skill is able to do.

   For *knowledge or concept* types of training, focus on learner's understanding of processes and structures. Use analogies and case studies to enhance the relevance of the material. Explain how the new concepts will be important to the participants in their work, using specific company examples when possible.

5. *Check Knowledge.* Continually check for understanding; make certain the participants both hear and understand the material as you present it. Are they now ready to apply it? Did they reach the appropriate level of understanding, according to the objectives? To decide, ask specific questions about the content you've just presented and demonstrated. When participants respond, tell them if their response is correct or not. When a response is not correct, help them understand what the correct response should have been.

6. *Practice.* Give the learners the chance to practice or use the new skill or knowledge. This often requires direct instructor feedback, though some skill training provides its own feedback. (For example, when the learner enters the wrong command on a computer, feedback from the program will normally indicate that it was wrong.)

7. *Evaluation.* Check what the learners have learned. Once the individual practice is complete, the participants are ready to begin or return to their jobs, unless additional skills or knowledge are part of the training plan. Once all the training has been completed, be sure to include assessments of the program as a whole.

See Worksheets 5–1 and 5–2 for suggested end-of-module and end-of-program evaluation forms. You may also modify them to add, change, or delete questions, to better serve the purpose of evaluation in your organization.

How Is Business Training Different From an Academic Setting?

Because of the many differences, teaching decision making in a business setting should not be handled the same way as teaching science in high school. Table 4–1 highlights many of these distinctions.

Table 4–1

Differences Between Academic Learning and Organizational Training

FACTOR	ACADEMIC LEARNING	ORGANIZATIONAL TRAINING
Trainer or teacher credentials	Academic achievement is often the sole criteria, although some colleges, especially two-year and teaching schools, will also consider work experience and the teacher's skills in interpersonal communications.	Skill or knowledge in the relevant subject, regardless of academic achievement; skill in interpersonal communications will also be more critical.
Course content	Content is usually broad and theoretical; certain fields such as computer science may also have a practical element.	Content is focused and application-oriented; it deals mostly with facts and procedures and only rarely with concepts.
Objectives	The most common objectives are knowledge-based and occasionally skill-based; job performance objectives are usually only a peripheral issue.	Although training often includes knowledge and skill-level objectives, job performance is the outcome of most concern.
Timing and scheduling	The schedule is usually lock step and tied to a semester or quarter system.	The schedule is typically short-term and more self-paced; new groups start as needed.
Grading system	Grades are typically "A" through "F."	Many programs are not graded at all, but are usually pass-fail; some are proficiency-based.
Presentation style	Lecture and other inductive forms are common, though workshops and lab applications may be used.	Participative (interactive) experiences are often used, even in a classroom form; a hands-on format is most common for on-the-job training.

continued on next page

Table 4–1, continued
Differences Between Academic Learning and Organizational Training

FACTOR	ACADEMIC LEARNING	ORGANIZATIONAL TRAINING
Reason for participation	The goal is to obtain a degree, certificate, or other credential; sometimes classes are taken for self-satisfaction, but usually for career and employment reasons.	Participants are usually required to attend training by employer to support the organization's needs; it may be a condition of keeping their job or getting a promotion.
Students or learners	Students work as individuals, and working together on assignments may be considered cheating; the teacher's "client" is the individual student.	Group learning is common; the trainer's "client" is the organization in which the participant works.
Learning or training materials	Comprehensive textbooks and outside research materials are used.	Company materials and trainer-designed materials are used; although books may be used, it is rare.

© 2004 Robert H. Vaughn

What Else Can I Do to Make the Content Understandable?

Here are some ways that you can improve the knowledge transfer for your participants.

Ask Frequent Questions. Design the lesson so that the material is grouped in bite-sized chunks. Don't just lecture for half an hour and then ask for questions. Learners should go through a questioning cycle every five to eight minutes.

Present information in a variety of ways: by lecture, demonstrations, and exercises, or with visuals or anything else that affects one or more of the senses of the learners. Then, to find out if what you've presented has been heard, seen, understood, and accepted, you need to elicit feedback from the learners in some way. The final part of a questioning cycle is letting the participants know if they've "got it."

Use Variety in the Training Design. Have the learners get up from their seats and move around occasionally, to talk with each other or try an experiment or exercise. Use more than one style to present the material. Three or four different approaches—perhaps a lecture, a discussion, a slide presentation, and an exercise—in a half-day session will help keep participants involved and learning.

Over-plan. First-time trainers are sometimes badly surprised when their planned one-hour presentation is completed in only 14 minutes. Even worse yet, sometimes it's not completed in 90 minutes.

Experienced trainers agree that it pays to over-prepare and that it's a good idea to practice a new training program in a dry run with a video recorder and a timer.

Be sure to have some contingency plans, especially if the training plan is deductive or interactive. Know what can be skimmed over or skipped completely if the training is running longer than planned, and keep an eye on the clock when time is a concern. Have extra material or additional exercises available if training runs short, or just let class out early, if it is appropriate to do so *and* if the training objectives have been met.

Ask for Help. A number of sources inside and outside your organization may be able to suggest ideas to improve the training. Talk with people who have taught similar programs. Valuable professional contacts may be found in such organizations as the local chapter of ASTD, the International Society for Performance Improvement (ISPI), or others. Even the participants may be willing to lend a hand in certain parts of the training where they have personal experience.

How Do I Encourage Participation? Unless you are lecturing or using some other one-way process from start to finish, you'll need participation by the class. When you encourage participation, take care to make it a challenging but nonthreatening experience. Participants don't mind training that is challenging, but they don't like to be embarrassed in front of their peers. They also learn more if they are involved. Here are some suggestions to get responses and involvement from your participants:

- ◆ *Use small groups.* Most people are more participative in small groups than in large classes.

- ◆ *Ask questions that can be answered by everyone.* Especially ask short-answer questions. You can also ask for a show of hands on some issues.

- ◆ *Use written exercises.* Having everyone write down an answer to questions allows you to go around the room and see if people are learning. Discuss any misconceptions or gaps in knowledge, which show up as a result of the exercise.

◆ *Call on people.* Ask direct questions of individuals. It's good practice to not call on the same people again and again, even if they are first to put up their hands. Instead, distribute the responsibility of answering among all the participants. Wait a while (at least 10 seconds) before choosing whom to call on, to let some people continue their thinking process. If you're pushed for time and want to find out if people know specific facts or procedures, ask closed questions, which have only one correct answer. If you want more discussion, to see whether the learners understand concepts, ask open-ended questions, which invite longer answers and may go in a number of different directions.

◆ *Give feedback.* Let them know how they're doing or what they need to do differently. Positive feedback is always appreciated, but not always possible. If you must give negative feedback, try to consider the sensitivity of the individual involved. Some people will accept "you're wrong," better than others, who need to hear, "that's not quite right."

◆ *Ask them what they think.* Participants learn from their peers, and critiques or support from others in the class may be more significant than agreement by the trainer.

◆ *Remember that lack of responsiveness doesn't necessarily indicate a lack of understanding.* Reasons for not responding can include insecurity, fatigue, passive-aggressive behavior, or many other things. It could be that you need to rephrase the question. Of course, it could also be that participants haven't yet learned what you're teaching, and you need to go over it again.

How Can I Effectively Use Subgroups and Peer Training?

Using subgroups in a training program has many advantages for both the participants and the trainer. Many adults are quite willing to learn from each other, and they may feel less threatened by their peers than by the trainer, especially if the trainer is an outsider. Peers may be better able to put new ideas and skills into the language and context of the workplace, thus making it easier for participants to apply the new knowledge to their jobs.

When peers help others in the class, they refine their own abilities and knowledge as they explain things to their peers. Teaching provides them an intrinsic reward, as well. The trainer who uses groups reaps an additional benefit: Fewer people are vying for his or her attention. This can provide time to catch your breath or deal with administrative items such as setting up equipment or reviewing lesson plans—or a few minutes of quiet time.

Using groups in training sessions also has risks. Groups may make it easier for individual participants to "hide," as their peers cover for them or let them be "free riders" on the backs of others in the group. Also, negative group dynamics may get in the way of effective learning if personalities or other issues keep the group from functioning properly.

For short questions, groups of two ("turn to your neighbor") is quick and practical. Groups of three might provide more richness or work better in situations where you need an observer (such as role plays). Larger groups of four to six may be good for case studies, but the instructor may need to provide more structure, such as having the group elect a spokesperson, giving specific roles to different people, and so on. It's often a good idea to mix up the groups at least daily so varying strengths and weakness of individual participants can be controlled, and so disparities in group levels don't become exacerbated.

How Do I Wrap Up the Program?

Although first impressions are important, so are the last impressions. As the training comes to an end, a variety of tasks need to be accomplished.

- *Have something meaningful to do.* All of your training should be meaningful, but it's good to end with a significant task that people can feel good about.

- *Remind people what they've learned.* Recap the training by referring to the schedule or the training objectives. Make sure to tie all the parts together and emphasize how the newly acquired knowledge and skills can be used back on the job.

- *Create action plans.* Whenever possible, have the participants put into writing how they plan to use the new knowledge or skills they have acquired. Some trainers keep these statements and mail them to the learners later, as a reminder or reinforcement technique.

◆ *Complete administrative requirements.* These could include administering a posttest knowledge check or skills test, handing out and collecting the program evaluations, getting any documentation signed or distributed (such as certificates of completion), and so on.

◆ *Prepare the participants for any follow-up.* Make sure the learners are aware of what will be expected of them after training. Will the participants be asked to fill out any other documents once they return to their jobs? Will they be subject to a follow-up evaluation by their supervisors or by others? Will they be asked to participate in any further training?

What to Do Next

Consider what you will do to "plan to succeed":

◆ Review chapters 6, 7, and 8 to decide which combination of training modules best fits the needs of your organization or the time available.

◆ Develop your lesson plans using chapters 9 through 18, as appropriate.

◆ Once your lesson plans are laid out, review the issues in this chapter point by point, to see where you might incorporate each of the ideas.

◆

Evaluating the Workshop

What's in This Chapter?

- ◆ Reasons for evaluation

- ◆ Explanations of evaluation techniques and instruments and how they are used

Reasons for Evaluation of Training

Business guru Tom Peters tells us, "What gets measured gets done. . . . Even imperfect measures provide a strategic indication of progress or lack thereof." The evaluation of training is an essential process to ensure that the organization's resources are being used wisely. Evaluation is important to the organization, as well as to the trainer and the participants. Organizations will want to know: "Is the cost of training justified?" Trainers will want to know, "How successful have I been in doing my job?" Participants will want assurances that they have been successful in their learning efforts and will be able to effectively perform their jobs.

Two different, yet related, meanings are attached to the concept of evaluation as related to training.

- ◆ Has the participant *learned the content* according to the specified training objectives?

- ◆ Was the *process* by which that learning occurred effective and appropriate?

In the training business, the generally accepted model for discussing evaluation of learning was developed in the late 1950s by Donald Kirkpatrick. He uses four levels of evaluation:

- ◆ Level 1: Reaction

- ◆ Level 2: Learning

- ◆ Level 3: Behavior

- ◆ Level 4: Results

Each of these measures can be applied only to training objectives that were written to those levels. For example, if the objective is that the learners will "understand how to use a decision matrix," that's a Level 2 objective and can be measured by asking them to explain how to use it. A Level 3 objective, for example, "Participants will be able to create a decision matrix," must be measured by having the participant actually create a decision matrix (not just explain how to create one).

Evaluating at the Reaction Level

Trainers almost always use an end-of-course evaluation form to obtain a rating of how the participants liked the program, what they gained most from it, and other information related to the training. An ASTD/i4cp research report, *The Value of Evaluation*, found that about 90 percent of organizations evaluate training at this level. These Level 1 evaluations are sometimes ironically referred to in the training industry as "smile sheets."

The reaction-level evaluations may include questions about both content and process. The fact is, at this lowest level, content and process may be somewhat difficult to separate. Because the only practical and immediate way to determine if an attitude or awareness has changed as a result of training is to simply ask the participants, it is common to ask their opinion on both content and process on the same form. Although such analysis is obviously open to significant bias, it still can serve a valid purpose.

Reaction-level evaluations can be done at any time during training, or months after it is over, not only at the conclusion of the last training session. When it's possible to change the training program while it is underway or if remedial training is an option, daily feedback may help a trainer adjust the training to better meet the needs of the learners or of the next group to be trained.

A word of caution about the interpretation of results from a Level 1 evaluation: Level 1 evaluations tend to be positively biased. Interestingly, whether participants did well in the training or not turns out to be a non-issue. If the delivery of the training was seen to be "good" or at least "adequate," then high satisfaction and low dissatisfaction among the participants were assured. Ironically, even if delivery was not adequate, there was still a better than 50 percent chance that participants would report high satisfaction and low dissatisfaction. Evaluations of training via Kirkpatrick's first (reaction) level, therefore, are of the most value in (1) providing a means of bringing closure to the class, and (2) providing narrative comments that may be useful to the trainer. Overall, however, they may tell us very little about what the participant really learned and frequently tell us nothing about either the content or process of the training.

The materials available with this book include Level 1 evaluation forms. The questions deal with both the content (that is, decision making) and the process by which the training was delivered. Adapt these suggested evaluations to better match the way your training is actually conducted.

Evaluating Learning at the Learning Level

Learning-level (Level 2) assessment is typically done by oral or written testing. Evaluation options include using true-false, matching, multiple choice, fill-in-the-blank, short answer, and essay questions, along with variations in each. Any of these formats could be given orally, in writing, or by using an interactive medium.

Most people have taken hundreds of tests in their lifetime and could probably deductively critique most testing formats. Knowledge testing is a complex topic. Anyone with further interest in the subject should refer to books on the subject (see For Further Reading).

Although much easier to do than Level 3 or Level 4 testing, knowledge testing can be deceptive. Properly done, knowledge testing measures learning and retention of the facts and processes addressed in the training. But it does not measure whether people are actually going to use the knowledge or whether it benefits the organization in any way.

A selection of Level 2 questions for evaluating decision-making training has been included in the materials with this book. Modify the questions to reflect the material actually covered in your training sessions.

Evaluating Learning on a Behavioral Level

Behavioral evaluations (Level 3) are related to objectives that demand practical skills. Evaluation requires actual performance of the skill to demonstrate that it has been learned and that the participant can apply the skill. Behavior level evaluations may occur either during the training, in the form of skill tests, or on-the-job, following training. In some cases, posttesting should be delayed, perhaps as much as several months.

A selection of Level 3 decision-making exercises, which can be done during the training, are included in the course materials. However, evaluation of actual on-the-job behavior cannot be done during the training and is difficult to document (especially for a subject like decision making) at any time, even by supervisors or participants.

This leads to another important point about evaluations, especially regarding "results level" evaluations (Level 4). Sometimes, even when the participant has developed and used the skill on the job, it does not make any difference to the organization's bottom line. That's what Kirkpatrick's fourth level is designed to measure: Has the training made a difference to the organization?

Evaluating Learning on a Results Level

The purpose of training in an organization is to enhance results. Training happens because the organization needs the learners to know or do something better, faster, or smarter than they would have been able to do without training. The reason for evaluating at this level is to show how the training has affected business results. Level 4 evaluations are usually conducted some time—maybe even months—after the training to give the learners time to use the new skills on the job.

Beyond Level 4, some organizations may choose to evaluate *return-on-investment.* These return-on-investment (ROI) evaluations require skills (such as accounting and economics techniques) that are not necessarily associated with the training profession. The evaluator may need to deal with financial records, market analyses, industrial engineering techniques, and sometimes even the psychological and cultural aspects of organizational operations. For further information on how to do this kind of evaluation, see work by Jack Phillips or Robert Brinkerhoff. Because of the complex nature of ROI evaluations, no means of doing these are included in this training package.

Evaluation Instruments Provided in this Book

A typical Level 1 evaluation form (Evaluation Instrument 5–1) is included at the end of this chapter and also on the website as a separate file, which can be downloaded and modified. A different evaluation form may be used as the end-of-program evaluation; it is shown at the end of this chapter as Evaluation Instrument 5–2.

Level 2 assessment questions and answers (tied to the various training objectives specified in the modules) are located at the end of each chapter. You are welcome to use them as provided or modify them to meet your needs.

Level 3 assessments are an intrinsic part of the worksheets and application exercises, which are provided in separate files. They can be tied to the skill objectives for each module.

What to Do Next

◆ Review the evaluation instruments provided with the modules.

◆ Decide what, if any, questions should be added or removed to meet requirements or needs of your organization.

Evaluation Instrument 5–1
Level 1 Evaluation Form

Please indicate your response by circling one number for each of the items below. Place this evaluation face down on the front desk as you leave. Thank you.

ABOUT THE EXPERIENCE	RATING LOW — HIGH	COMMENTS
Instructor's knowledge of subject matter	1 2 3 4 5	
Instructor's skill in training	1 2 3 4 5	
Effectiveness of the handout materials	1 2 3 4 5	
Effectiveness of the visuals	1 2 3 4 5	
Learning value of the exercises	1 2 3 4 5	
Comfort of the facilities	1 2 3 4 5	
Adequacy of the preliminary arrangements	1 2 3 4 5	
Overall evaluation of the training program	1 2 3 4 5	

ABOUT THE SUBJECT MATTER	RATING LOW — HIGH	COMMENTS
Amount of information I learned as a result of this training	1 2 3 4 5	
Usefulness of this training to me on my job	1 2 3 4 5	
My level of knowledge about this subject prior to today's training	1 2 3 4 5	
Difficulty I had in understanding this material. (*Note*: 5 = a lot of difficulty.)	5 4 3 2 1	

What two things were most beneficial to you from this session?
1
2

What improvements would you suggest in this training program?

Evaluation Instrument 5–2
Final Full-Program Evaluation Form

Please indicate your response by circling one number for each of the items below. Place this evaluation face down on the front desk as you leave. Thank you.

ABOUT THE EXPERIENCE	RATING LOW HIGH	COMMENTS
Instructor's knowledge of subject matter	1 2 3 4 5	
Instructor's skill in training	1 2 3 4 5	
Effectiveness of the worksheet materials	1 2 3 4 5	
Effectiveness of the visuals	1 2 3 4 5	
Learning value of the exercises	1 2 3 4 5	
Comfort of the facilities	1 2 3 4 5	
Adequacy of the preliminary arrangements	1 2 3 4 5	
Overall evaluation of the training program	1 2 3 4 5	

ABOUT THE SUBJECT MATTER	RATING LOW HIGH	COMMENTS
Amount of information I learned as a result of this training	1 2 3 4 5	
Likelihood that I will be make better decisions as a result of this training	1 2 3 4 5	
My level of knowledge about decision making prior to this training program	1 2 3 4 5	
What three things were most beneficial to you from this program?	1 2 3	
What two things from this training program were least useful to you?	1 2	

Other comments can be made on the back of the form.

Section Three:
Training Program Agendas

◆

Half-Day Program

- ◆ Overview of modules used for a half-day training session

- ◆ Description of a half-day program, objectives, and modules to be used

- ◆ Topics covered and time needed to present modules

The half-day workshop provides an overview of the decision-making process and will enable the learners to grasp and use some of the key concepts of the process.

Overview of Modules Presented

A half-day session consists of:

Module 1—The Decision-Making Process: Anatomy of a Decision (Ch 9)

Module 2—The Creative Process: Developing Options (Ch 10)

Module 6—The Analytic Process: Narrowing Down the Options (Ch 14)

Module 9—The Human Aspect: Emotional and Irrational Factors (Ch 17)

Use a combination of module 1 and module 9 in programs for managers and supervisors who already know some of the tools and techniques related to creativity and analysis. You'll begin with the overview and focus on the human aspects, which aren't necessarily covered in other management skills courses.

For a general audience, use a combination of module 1, module 2, and module 6 to give participants a more complete picture of the decision-making process, although realize that those modules don't cover all of the tools and human aspects of decision making.

Presented below is an overview of the four suggested modules for a half-day workshop, along with the training objectives and a sample agenda with approximate time needed to complete the modules. Please refer to chapters 9, 10, 14, and 17 for the full module contents, which include a detailed trainer's guide for use with each module.

How to Present the Modules

Present the modules in the following order for a half-day training session:

- ◆ Managers and supervisors—Begin with module 1 and then follow up with module 9.

- ◆ General audience—Begin with module 1, follow with module 2, and end with module 6.

Module 1—The Decision-Making Process: Anatomy of a Decision (Ch 9)

Module 1 introduces the subject of decision making and presents a framework that will be used throughout the program.

TRAINING OBJECTIVES

After completing this module, the participants should be able to

- ◆ list and explain the steps by which a decision is made

- ◆ explain the benefits of a structured decision-making process

- ◆ determine the relative importance of a decision.

MODULE 1 TIME

- ◆ Approximately 2 hours

Introduction and welcome; housekeeping items   15 minutes

Pretest and discussion   15 minutes

PowerPoint presentation	30 minutes
Break	10 minutes
Finish PowerPoint presentation	10 minutes
Handout/worksheet and discussion	30 minutes
Wrap-up, learning check, and preview	10 minutes

Note: This time estimate includes a pretest, a learning check at the end, and time for the administrative items associated with starting a training program, such as individual introductions, laying out the schedule and ground rules, and so on. A break is included in modules of more than 90 minutes.

Module 2—The Creative Process: Developing Options (Ch 10)

Module 2 introduces the subjects of creativity and risk in decision making.

TRAINING OBJECTIVES

After completing this module, the participants should be able to

- explain the importance of creativity in decision making

- clarify the goal of a decision

- develop or identify viable options from which to choose

- calculate the degree of risk related to a decision.

MODULE 2 TIME

- Approximately 1 hour

Introduction, welcome, and review	5 minutes
PowerPoint presentation	30 minutes
Worksheet/exercise and discussion	20 minutes
Wrap-up, learning check, and preview	5 minutes

Note: This includes time for a quick review and a learning check at the end.

Module 6—The Analytic Process: Narrowing Down the Options (Ch 14)

Module 6 covers the subject of gathering information to help make an effective decision.

TRAINING OBJECTIVES

After completing this module, the participants should be able to

- ◆ identify significant sources of data for decision-making analysis

- ◆ determine the value of collecting additional information

- ◆ explain and use the concept of Pareto analysis.

MODULE 6 TIME

- ◆ Approximately 1 hour

Review prior modules and introduction of module 6	5 minutes
PowerPoint presentation and discussion	30 minutes
Worksheet/exercise	20 minutes
Wrap-up, measurement, and preview	5 minutes

Note: This includes time for a quick review at the start and a learning check at the end.

Module 9—The Human Aspect: Emotional and Irrational Factors (Ch 17)

Module 9 covers the human aspects of making decisions.

TRAINING OBJECTIVES

After completing this module, participants should be able to

- ◆ discuss the merits of group versus individual decision-making

- ◆ list at least two differences between expert and layperson decision-making

- ◆ describe the influence of framing on the decision-making process

- ◆ describe the influence of technology on the decision-making process.

MODULE 9 TIME

◆ Approximately 1.5 hours

Review and introduction of module 9	5 minutes
PowerPoint presentation and discussion	60 minutes
Worksheet/exercise	20 minutes
Wrap-up, measurement, and preview	5 minutes

Note: This estimate includes time for a quick review at the start and a learning check at the end.

What to Do Next

◆ Review the contents of chapters 9, 10, 14, and 17 as appropriate, and decide which (if any) of the suggested elements you do not need to include. You may choose to rearrange, edit, or combine the material to best meet your organization's specific training needs. For example, you should exclude topics that your participants already understand at a high-enough level.

◆ Decide whether there is any other content relevant to your organization that you wish to add. You may want to include additional information in your presentations, in the worksheets, or in the visuals that tailor the content to your organization, industry, or a specific group's requirements.

◆ Go to the website www.astd.org/decisionmakingtraining and download the PowerPoint slides, worksheets, and any other materials you will need.

◆ Modify the PowerPoint slides by adding background, company logo, or other enhancements, such as different transitions, sound, and so forth, to match your presentation requirements.

◆

Full-Day Program

- ◆ Overview of modules used for a full-day training session

- ◆ Description of the program, objectives, and modules used in a full-day program

- ◆ Topics covered and the time needed to present the modules

The full-day (or one-day) program employs an optimum combination of information that hits the high points of the decision-making process. To provide variety in a solid day of training, the full-day program includes many opportunities for participants to play an active role in the program and provides chances to move away from inductive (lecture only) training.

The full-day workshop provides an overview of the decision-making process and will enable the learners to grasp and use some of the key concepts of the process. These training modules are used for the full-day training session:

Module 1—The Decision-Making Process: Anatomy of a Decision (Ch 9)

Module 2—The Creative Process: Developing Options (Ch 10)

Module 5—Tools to Improve Creativity (Ch 13)

Module 6—The Analytic Process: Narrowing Down the Options (Ch 14)

Module 8—Using Tools to Improve Analysis (Ch 16)

Module 9—The Human Aspect: Emotional and Irrational Factors (Ch 17)

Overview of Modules to Be Presented

Presented below is an overview of the suggested modules for a full-day workshop, including the training objectives and a sample agenda with the approximate time needed to complete each module. Please refer to chapters 9, 10, 13, 14, 16, and 17 for the module contents and a detailed facilitator's guide for each module.

How to Present the Modules

In a full-day program, present the modules as follows:

- ◆ Managers and supervisors—Begin with module 1 and then go to modules 2, 6, 8, and 9. If your participants are familiar with decision-making analysis, skip module 8 and go to module 9.

- ◆ General audience or technicians—Begin with module 1, followed by modules 2, 5, 6, and 8.

Module 1—The Decision-Making Process: Anatomy of a Decision (Ch 9)

This is the first module in the training program and lays a foundation for all that follows. It introduces the subject of decision making and breaks it down into the process that will be used throughout the program.

TRAINING OBJECTIVES

After completing this module, the participants should be able to

- ◆ list and explain the steps by which a decision is made

- ◆ explain the benefits of a structured decision-making process

- ◆ determine the relative importance of a decision.

MODULE 1 TIME

- ◆ Approximately 2 hours

Introduction, welcome, and housekeeping items	15 minutes
Pretest and discussion	15 minutes

PowerPoint presentation and discussion	30 minutes
Break	10 minutes
Finish PowerPoint presentation	10 minutes
Worksheet/exercise and discussion	30 minutes
Wrap-up, learning check, and preview	10 minutes

Note: This includes time for a pretest at the start, a learning check at the end, and the typical administrative trivia associated with starting a training program (such as introductions, laying out the schedule and ground rules, and so on). A break is included in modules of more than 90 minutes.

Module 2—The Creative Process: Developing Options (Ch 10)

This module introduces the subjects of creativity and risk in decision making.

TRAINING OBJECTIVES

After completing this module, the participants should be able to

- explain the importance of creativity in decision making

- clarify the goals of a decision

- develop or identify viable options from which to choose

- calculate the degree of risk related to a decision.

MODULE 2 TIME

- Approximately 1 hour

Introduction, welcome, and review	5 minutes
PowerPoint presentation	30 minutes
Worksheet/exercise and discussion	20 minutes
Wrap-up, learning check, and preview	5 minutes

Note: This includes time for a quick review at the start and a learning check at the end.

Module 5—Tools to Improve Creativity (Ch 13)

Module 5 describes tools that can improve creativity.

TRAINING OBJECTIVES

After completing this module, the participants should be able to

- describe and use at least five simple tools that may help improve creativity

- apply the appropriate tools to a variety of situations requiring creativity.

MODULE 5 TIME

- Approximately 2 hours

Introduction, welcome, and review	5 minutes
Mixed PowerPoint and exercises	50 minutes
Break	10 minutes
Mixed PowerPoint and practice	50 minutes
Wrap-up, learning check, and preview	5 minutes

Note: This includes time for a quick review at the start and a learning check at the end. It also includes a constant back and forth from presentation of skills to application of skills. As with all modules of more than 90 minutes, a 10-minute break is included.

Module 6—The Analytic Process: Narrowing Down the Options (Ch 14)

Module 6 covers methods for gathering information to help make an effective decision.

TRAINING OBJECTIVES

After completing this module, the participants should be able to

- identify significant sources of data for decision-making analysis

- determine the value of collecting additional information

- explain and use the concept of Pareto analysis.

MODULE 6 TIME

- ◆ Approximately 1 hour

Review and introduction of the analytic process	5 minutes
PowerPoint presentation and discussion	30 minutes
Worksheet/exercise	20 minutes
Wrap-up, measurement, and preview	5 minutes

Note: This includes time for a quick review at the start and a learning check at the end.

Module 8—Using Tools to Improve Analysis (Ch 16)

Module 8 covers tools that are helpful when making decisions.

TRAINING OBJECTIVES

After completing this module, the participants should be able to

- ◆ describe at least five tools that may help improve analysis of information

- ◆ apply the appropriate tools to a variety of situations requiring analysis of information.

MODULE 8 TIME

- ◆ Approximately 2 hours

Review and introduction to tools for analyzing information	5 minutes
PowerPoint presentation and discussion	50 minutes
Break	10 minutes
Continue PowerPoint presentation	20 minutes
Practice/worksheets	30 minutes
Wrap-up, measurement, and preview	5 minutes

Note: This includes time for a quick review at the start and a learning check at the end. As do all modules of more than 90 minutes, the schedule includes time for a 10-minute break.

Module 9—The Human Aspect: Emotional and Irrational Factors (Ch 17)

Module 9 covers the human aspects of making decisions.

TRAINING OBJECTIVES

After completing this module, the participants should be able to

- ◆ discuss the merits of group decision making versus individual decision making

- ◆ list at least two differences between expert and layperson decision-making

- ◆ describe the influence of framing on the decision-making process

- ◆ describe the influence of technology on the decision-making process.

MODULE 9 TIME

- ◆ Approximately 1.5 hours

Review and introduction to the human aspects of decision making	5 minutes
PowerPoint presentation and discussion	60 minutes
Worksheet/exercise	20 minutes
Wrap-up and measurement	5 minutes

Note: This includes time for a quick review at the start and a learning check at the end.

What to Do Next

- ◆ Review the contents of chapters 9, 10, 13, 14, 16, and 17 as appropriate, and decide which (if any) of the suggested elements you do not need to include. You may choose to rearrange, edit, or combine the material to best meet your organization's specific training needs. For example, you should exclude topics that your participants already understand at a high-enough level.

◆ Decide whether there is any other content relevant to your organization that you wish to add. You may want to include additional information in your presentations, in the worksheets, or in the visuals that tailor the content to your organization, industry, or a specific group's requirements.

◆ Go to the website www.astd.org/decisionmakingtraining and download the PowerPoint slides, worksheets, and any other materials you will need.

◆ Modify the PowerPoint slides by adding background, company logo, or other enhancements, such as different transitions, sound, and so forth, to match your presentation requirements.

◆

Two-Day Program

What's in This Chapter?

- ◆ Overview of modules used for a two-day training session

- ◆ Description of the program, and the objectives and modules to be used

- ◆ Topics covered and time needed to present each module

The two-day workshop provides a comprehensive overview of the decision-making process and enables the learners to grasp and use all the key concepts of the process. These training modules are used for the two-day session:

Module 1—The Decision-Making Process: Anatomy of a Decision (Ch 9)

Module 2—The Creative Process: Developing Options (Ch 10)

Module 3—Barriers to Creativity (Ch 11)

Module 4—Overcoming Barriers to Creativity (Ch 12)

Module 5—Tools to Improve Creativity (Ch 13)

Module 6—The Analytic Process: Narrowing Down the Options (Ch 14)

Module 7—Using Everyday Statistics (Ch 15)

Module 8—Using Tools to Improve Analysis (Ch 16)

Module 9—The Human Aspect: Emotional and Irrational Factors (Ch 17)

Module 10—Implementing the Decision: Wrap-Up (Ch 18)

Overview of Modules Presented

Presented below is an overview of the modules for a two-day workshop, including the training objectives and a sample agenda with approximate times needed to complete each of the modules. Please refer to chapters 9 through 18 for a full description of the module contents, including a detailed facilitator's guide for each module.

Module 1—The Decision-Making Process: Anatomy of a Decision (Ch 9)

Module 1 lays a foundation for all that follows it. It introduces the subject of decision making and breaks it into the process that will be used throughout the training workshop.

TRAINING OBJECTIVES

After completing module 1, the participants should be able to

- list and explain the steps by which a decision is made

- explain the benefits of a structured decision-making process

- determine the relative importance of a decision.

MODULE 1 TIME

- Approximately 2 hours

Introduction, welcome, and housekeeping items	15 minutes
Pretest and discussion	15 minutes
PowerPoint presentation	30 minutes
Break	10 minutes
Complete PowerPoint presentation	10 minutes
Worksheet exercise and discussion	30 minutes
Wrap-up, learning check, and preview	10 minutes

Note: This schedule includes time for a pretest at the start, a learning check at the end, and administrative trivia associated with starting a training program (such as introductions, laying out the schedule and ground rules, and so on). A 10-minute break is included in modules of more than 90 minutes.

Module 2—The Creative Process: Developing Options (Ch 10)

Module 2 introduces the subjects of creativity and risk in decision making.

TRAINING OBJECTIVES

After completing module 2, the participants should be able to

- explain the importance of creativity in decision making
- clarify the goal of a decision
- develop or identify viable options from which to choose
- calculate the degree of risk related to a decision.

MODULE 2 TIME

- Approximately 1 hour

Introduction, welcome, and review	5 minutes
PowerPoint presentation	30 minutes
Worksheet/exercise and discussion	20 minutes
Wrap-up, learning check, and preview	5 minutes

Note: This includes time for a quick review at the start and a learning check at the end.

Module 3—Barriers to Creativity (Ch 11)

This module delves into the subject of barriers to creativity.

TRAINING OBJECTIVES

After completing module 3, the participants should be able to identify

- six kinds of barriers that may prevent effective decision making
- personal traits related to decision making
- factors to consider in group decision making.

MODULE 3 TIME

* Approximately 1 hour

Introduction, welcome, and review of previous modules	5 minutes
PowerPoint presentation	25 minutes
Creativity barriers exercise	15 minutes
Group discussions of barriers to creativity	10 minutes
Wrap-up, learning check, and preview of next module	5 minutes

Note: This includes time for a quick review and a learning check at the end.

Module 4—Overcoming Barriers to Creativity (Ch 12)

Module 4 presents methods for overcoming the barriers to creativity identified in module 3. Module 4 is recommended for any session in which the training program lasts more than one day. It should always follow module 3.

TRAINING OBJECTIVES

After completing module 4, the participants should be able to

* explain four techniques for overcoming barriers to decision making

* develop a personal plan for reducing at least two common barriers.

MODULE 4 TIME

* Approximately 1 hour

Introduction, welcome, and review of previous module	5 minutes
PowerPoint presentation and discussion	30 minutes
Worksheet/exercise	20 minutes
Wrap-up, learning check, and preview of next module	5 minutes

Note: This schedule includes time for a quick review at the start and a learning check at the end.

Module 5—Tools to Improve Creativity (Ch 13)

This module describes several tools that can help improve creativity.

TRAINING OBJECTIVES

After completing this module, the participants should be able to

- describe and use at least five tools that may help improve creativity

- apply the appropriate tools to a variety of situations requiring creativity.

MODULE 5 TIME

- Approximately 2 hours

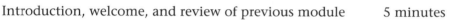

Introduction, welcome, and review of previous module	5 minutes
PowerPoint presentation and practice exercise	50 minutes
Break	10 minutes
PowerPoint presentation and practice exercise	50 minutes
Wrap-up, learning check, and preview of next module	5 minutes

Note: This schedule includes time for a quick review at the start and a learning check at the end. It includes time for both presentations by the trainer and exercises in applying new skills by participants. As with all units of more than 90 minutes, a 10-minute break is included.

Module 6—The Analytic Process: Narrowing Down the Options (Ch 14)

Module 6 covers the subject of gathering information to help make an effective decision.

TRAINING OBJECTIVES

After completing module 6, the participants should be able to

- identify significant sources of data for decision-making analysis

- determine the value of collecting additional information

- explain and use Pareto analysis.

MODULE 6 TIME

◆ Approximately 1 hour

Review and introduction of the analytic process	5 minutes
PowerPoint presentation and discussion	30 minutes
Worksheet/exercise	20 minutes
Wrap-up, measurement, and preview of next module	5 minutes

Note: This schedule includes time for a quick review at the start and a learning check at the end.

Module 7—Using Everyday Statistics (Ch 15)

Module 7 covers basic concepts of statistics that are helpful in making decisions.

Warn the boss about this module: On the chance that top brass in your organization may visit the training room, you may want to assure them that the card and dice games being played by participants are relevant to the subject of using statistics to improve decision making.

TRAINING OBJECTIVES

After completing this module, the participants should be able to

◆ define probability by using everyday examples

◆ use the concept of probability to explain simple gambling situations

◆ explain the process and uses of sampling data in decision making.

MODULE 7 TIME

◆ Approximately 1.5 hours

Review and introduction of statistical concepts	5 minutes
Exercise/games	15 minutes
PowerPoint presentation and discussion*	55 minutes
Practice exercise*	10 minutes
Wrap-up, measurement, and preview	5 minutes

You may either integrate the practice exercise and the lecture or save the practice time until after the PowerPoint presentation and discussion.

Note: This schedule includes time for a quick review at the start and a learning check at the end.

Module 8—Using Tools to Improve Analysis (Ch 16)

Module 8 covers the use of simple tools that may be helpful when making decisions.

TRAINING OBJECTIVES

After completing module 8, the participants should be able to

- describe at least five tools that may help improve analysis of information

- apply the appropriate tools to a variety of situations requiring analysis of information.

MODULE 8 TIME

- Approximately 2 hours

Review and introduction of tools that improve analysis	5 minutes
PowerPoint presentation and discussion	50 minutes
Break	10 minutes
Complete PowerPoint presentation	20 minutes
Practice/worksheets	30 minutes
Wrap-up, measurement, and preview of next module	5 minutes

Note: This schedule includes time for a quick review at the start and a learning check at the end. As for all modules of more than 90 minutes, this schedule includes a 10-minute break.

Module 9—The Human Aspect: Emotional and Irrational Factors (Ch 17)

Module 9 covers the human aspects that frequently arise in making decisions.

TRAINING OBJECTIVES

After completing this module, the participants should be able to

- ◆ discuss the merits of group versus individual decision-making processes

- ◆ list at least two differences between expert and layperson decision-making requirements

- ◆ describe the influence of framing on the decision-making process

- ◆ describe the influence of technology on the decision-making process.

MODULE 9 TIME

- ◆ Approximately 1.5 hours

Review and introduction of human aspects of decision making	5 minutes
PowerPoint presentation and discussion	60 minutes
Worksheet/exercise	20 minutes
Wrap-up, measurement, and preview of next module	5 minutes

Note: This schedule includes time for a quick review at the start and a learning check at the end.

Module 10—Implementing the Decision: Wrap-Up (Ch 18)

Module 10 describes a process for developing a proposal to elicit agreement to implement a decision. It should be used in all two-day programs. Module 10 also includes the end-of-program review and a posttest covering the material.

TRAINING OBJECTIVES

After completing this module, the participants should be able to

- ◆ list the important factors to consider in planning to implement a decision

- ◆ develop a plan for implementing a decision.

MODULE 10 TIME

- ◆ Approximately 2 hours

Review and introduction of tools for implementing a decision	5 minutes
PowerPoint presentation and discussion	40 minutes
Break	10 minutes
Evaluation Instrument	35 minutes
Posttest, discussion, and wrap-up	30 minutes

Note: This schedule includes time for a quick review at the start and a learning check at the end. As with all modules of more than 90 minutes, a 10-minute break is included. Because this is the final module, it includes time for a posttest and program evaluation (Evaluation Instrument 5–2).

What to Do Next

- ◆ Review the contents of chapters 9 through 18, as appropriate, and decide which (if any) of the suggested elements you do not need to include. You may choose to rearrange, edit, or combine the material to best meet your organization's specific training needs. For example, you should exclude topics that your participants already understand at a high-enough level.

- ◆ Decide whether there is any other content relevant to your organization that you wish to add. You may want to include additional information in your presentations, in the worksheets, or in the visuals that tailor the content to your organization, industry, or a specific group's requirements.

- ◆ Go to the website www.astd.org/decisionmakingtraining and download the PowerPoint slides, worksheets, and any other materials you will need.

- ◆ Modify the PowerPoint slides by adding background, company logo, or other enhancements, such as different transitions, sound, and so forth, to match your presentation requirements.

Section Four:
Learning Modules

Module 1—The Decision-Making Process: Anatomy of a Decision

This is the first module in the decision-making training program. It lays a foundation for all that follows by introducing the subject of decision making and breaking it apart into the process that will be used for the training. It should be used with programs of any length and can also be used as a stand-alone.

Training Objectives

After completing this module, the participants should be able to

- list and explain the steps by which a decision is made

- explain the benefits of a structured decision-making process

- determine the relative importance of a decision.

Module Time

- Approximately 2 hours

Note: The estimate of two hours includes time for a pretest, a learning check at the end, and time for the typical administrative tasks associated with starting a training program, such as individual introductions, laying out the schedule and ground rules, and so on. As in all modules of 90 minutes or more, a break is included.

Materials

- Attendance list

- Pencils, pens, and paper for each participant

- Whiteboard or flipchart and markers

◆ Name tags or name tents for each participant

◆ Worksheet 9–1: Icebreaker

◆ Worksheet 9–2: Decision Analysis Sheet

◆ Evaluation Instrument 9–1: Pretest on Decision Making

◆ Computer, screen, and projector for displaying PowerPoint slides; alternatively, overhead projector and overhead transparencies

◆ PowerPoint slide program (slides 9–1 through 9–22)

◆ This chapter for reference or detailed facilitator notes

◆ Optional: music, coffee or other refreshments.

Module Preparation

Arrive ahead of time to greet the participants and make sure materials are available and laid out to support the way you want to run the class. Test any computer equipment you will use in the session.

In chapter 2 you will find a needs analysis questionnaire (Worksheet 2–1). The needs analysis is optional but may be helpful to you as the trainer.

If participants have not filled out the questionnaire before this first session, you may wish to add 15 minutes to the agenda to allow time to present the questionnaire and have the participants fill it out. The timing as described below does *not* include the needs analysis.

Sample Agenda

0:00   Welcome class.

Have slide 9–1 on screen as people arrive; go to slide 9–2 as you begin.

Introduce yourself.

Take care of housekeeping items (information on schedule, restrooms, expectations).

Ask participants to introduce themselves or use Worksheet 9–1: Icebreaker (optional).

Review agenda for the entire program.

Ask for questions or concerns.

0:15   Pretest.

Distribute Evaluation Instrument 9–1: Pretest on Decision Making and allow 5 minutes maximum.

Display slide 9–3 as the participants complete the pretest, then show slide 9–4.

Slide 9–5 has the answers to the pretest. Discuss as group.

0:30   PowerPoint (PPT) Presentation.

Begin with slide 9–6 (objectives) and proceed through slide 9–15. See notes in PowerPoint file.

1:00   Break.

1:10   Finish PPT.

Show slides 9–16 through 9–19.

See notes in PowerPoint file and information below.

1:20   Worksheets.

Distribute Worksheet 9–2: Decision Analysis Sheet.

Show slide 9–20 as participants complete the worksheet.

Move among participants to keep them on task.

Group discussion—participants discuss answers with others.

1:50   Wrap-up.

Show slide 9–21—a summary of the foregoing material.

Ask for questions.

Check learning (questions can be oral or printed—see below).

Close with slide 9–22.

Trainer's Notes

8:00 a.m. Welcome (15 minutes).

Show slide 9–1 as participants arrive. Welcome participants, introduce your-self, and take care of housekeeping items such as information on schedule and location of restrooms.

Show slide 9–2 and conduct participant introductions.

This can be done informally, or you may choose to distribute Worksheet 9–1: Icebreaker (optional). Instructions are part of the handout.

Discuss the purpose of workshop.

8:15 a.m. Pretest (15 minutes).

Show slide 9–3. Distribute Evaluation Instrument 9–1: Pretest on Decision Making and explain how to complete the handout pretest self-assessment. Directions are on the worksheet.

Before you show the answers to the pretest, display and read slide 9–4 to begin the class with a smile.

Show slide 9–5. Discuss the answers to the pretest/self-assessment.

8:30 a.m. The Decision-Making Process (30 minutes).

Show slide 9–6 and discuss the learning objectives for the class.

Show slide 9–7.

You might want to ask the participants the question before you show them the three reasons and see what they come up with. The pretest question 9 about making decisions in the "right way" is relevant to this discussion. Don't just read the slide to them—you should paraphrase and discuss the points.

Show slide 9–8. Mention that Steven Covey is one of the best-selling business management authors of all time. Discuss why his statement is important.

Show slide 9–9, which illustrates the steps in the decision-making process. Point out to the class that you will be going through the entire decision-making process in more detail, but that the structure outlined on slide 9–9 is the basis for most of the rest of the training program. Allow participants time to copy down the steps. (Kinesthetic-learner types, as well as visual and auditory types, will appreciate your suggestion.) You might also have the steps in a handout.

Show slide 9–10. Step 1: Determine That a Decision Is Needed.

Decisions are needed if actions are to happen in an orderly way. If you are responsible for making something happen, you must make decisions. Here are good questions to ask at this point:

Does it have to be decided?—What will happen if no decision is made? (Often the answer is that nothing bad will happen.) What pros and cons are there for inaction? Sometimes when minor issues are ignored, they die a natural death and . . . *no one cares*. If that's the case, you can save yourself time and energy by not deciding.

Do I have the authority and power to make and implement the decision?—If not, why are you involved? Perhaps your reason for being involved is to recommend a course of action to someone else. Many staff people find themselves in this situation.

Do I have or can I get the necessary information to make the decision?—If not, you may as well throw a dart at a board listing all the choices. No use agonizing over it if there's really no way to get the information that will tell you which of your options is best.

Who else could make the decision better?—If there is someone, why not let him or her make the decision?

Show slide 9–11. Step 2: Determine the Importance of the Decision.

Decisions vary in importance: Dressing for a major job interview or social affair probably takes more thought than dressing to wash the car or the dog. Buying a house is a more important decision than buying socks.

Competent people intuitively know which decisions are important enough to merit more detailed processing (such as the process described in steps 3 through 7).

Most of us, however, know people who have difficulty making distinctions among the decisions they face—people who make all decisions seem equally important. These people usually frustrate themselves and others by agonizing over trivial decisions. You might say to the class that you will leave the analysis of why some people have this problem to specialists in human behavior. But for now, the class will consider the criteria most people use subconsciously to determine how important a decision is to them:

How much does it cost?—Importance usually increases with cost.

How long is the commitment?—Importance usually increases with the length of time with which one will have to endure the choice.

Who is involved?—Importance usually increases directly with the number of people involved and significance to the decision maker.

Can it be changed later?—Importance usually increases when it will be difficult or impossible to change the decision at a later time.

How soon does the decision have to be made?—Urgency and accompanying stress usually increase as the deadline nears. In one sense, then, importance may also increase. However, a decision may be urgent but still not very important. For example, the store may be closing. Do I need black or gray socks?

How much information is available to make the decision?—Although the information available may not directly influence the importance of the decision, it is a consideration. Either extreme—too much or not enough information—can increase stress.

Occasionally, however, we all goof in our estimation of a decision's importance. We may think a decision is unimportant when it really is important, or vice versa. This usually happens because we weren't aware of or didn't pay attention to all the data. Of course, sometimes things change after we've begun the decision-making process.

Ask the class to think back to decision(s) they wrote down on the pretest. How do the points just discussed apply to those decisions? Allow them a minute or so to reflect quietly.

Show slide 9–12. Step 3: Assess What Limits Apply to the Decision.

Limits are usually defined in terms of resources available: time, money, people, and so on. It's important to know these limits at the start, so the final decision takes those limits into account. Otherwise, the decision may not work.

Limits, also called parameters or conditions, are usually stated in terms of what resources the decision maker or the management of the organization is willing and able to apply toward achievement of the objectives. Therefore, when defining limits, you need to ask certain questions:

- ◆ How much time before the goal should be reached?

- ◆ How much money can be put toward its achievement?

- ◆ What equipment or facilities are available?

- ◆ What technological capabilities can be tapped?

- ◆ What people can be used? What technical and managerial skills do they have?

- ◆ What other resources are necessary?

- ◆ What will affect progress toward the goal?

The purpose of thinking through the limits is to reduce the number of options to be considered in the next step. For example, if your objective is to travel from Cincinnati to Chicago, you could do this in millions of ways. You could go by car, bicycle, plane, train, bus, or canoe. You could go through Indianapolis or Seattle or Paris.

By listing the limits before considering those routes, you reduce the pool of options to a practical number that can ultimately be viable. You could list other limits such as (1) getting there within one day and (2) having your own car to drive upon arrival. This, then, would limit your choice of options to fairly direct highway routes.

An important word of caution goes with this step: **Don't overdo the limits!** Too many limits can reduce the potential for more creative options. Also, too strict limits may force you to focus too early toward some conscious or unconscious preconceived "best way" to accomplish your goal.

You need to set limits, but only those that are essential and absolute. For example, if above you say "**MY** car," rather than "**A** car," you've limited yourself much more. If you just need "a car" upon arrival, then going by plane, train, boat, or hitchhiking are still realistic options if you buy, rent, or borrow a car in Chicago. They might also be better or cheaper options, even with the additional cost of getting a car in Chicago.

Show slide 9–13. Step 4: Determine Possible Choices.

Step 4 is the very important *inductive* or creative part of the planning process. It must be done effectively—that is, you must come up with a good list of options from which to choose—if you are to come up with an effective plan.

A discussion of ways you can develop creative options is part of a later module. However, two important points need to be covered here:

(1) Complete step 4 before you even think about step 5, and

(2) At this point you may not come up with *all* possible options. That's OK.

It is important to isolate step 4 from step 5. For one thing, the two steps use different sides of the brain. Creativity is generally associated with the right side of the brain, whereas analysis skills reside in the left side.

Further, many of the tools discussed later in this program are associated exclusively with one step or the other. Jumping back and forth between these steps adds unnecessary complications to the planning process.

Finally, human nature isn't always as patient as it should be. Flip-flopping between these steps will add time and probably increase pressures to cut the process short. The lesson is this: Don't start to evaluate the options until you've come up with an adequate list of options.

What is an "adequate" list? It is one that (a) has been developed with enough thought that you've included several different kinds of options. This may mean different vendors or locations or styles, and so forth. And (b) the differences between options should be more than just cosmetic. For example, if your house looks dreary, your options should not be only between brands of white paint. They should include various colors, stains, aluminum siding, and bricks. Of course, you might eliminate some of these in the next step, but at least consider them.

To illustrate the hazard of jumping to step 5 without first completing step 4, consider the process of planning to buy a car: *Objective*: To buy a car by this Friday. *Limits*: $18,000; room for five passengers; four-wheel drive; and so forth (add limits to meet your personal needs).

If you go to the first dealer's lot, see a car that fits the limits, and buy it without looking elsewhere, you may not have implemented the best plan. As you drive home in your new car, you may pass other dealerships and wonder if some of those cars might have been cheaper or better.

The other rule of thumb is not to go to step 5 until you have a minimum of four viable options. If four come fairly easily, go for a dozen. Use the car example again by noting that unless you live in a small town a long way from anywhere else you might buy a car, you'll probably not consider every possible option before you make a choice. Somewhere between dozens and thousands of cars are for sale in most places. It's neither possible nor logical to check out each and every one before you buy.

How many options are enough? It depends on the nature of the decision. A range of four to 12 options is adequate for most planning. Modules 2 through 5 will introduce you to a variety of ways to create a broader and more effective list of options.

Show slide 9–14. Step 5: Gather Information About the Choices.

Emphasize to the class that this step is the start of the ***deductive*** or data-gathering and analytical (that is, left brain) part of the decision-making process. Give an example by asking participants, "How many kinds of cookies are available in your local grocery store?" And ask them how much information can be obtained by reading the package of each kind of cookie. Finally, ask how a "logical" decision might be made with this information?

More about data collection will be covered in module 6, and more about the issues of too much information in module 9. *Note:* If your program will not include those modules, either don't mention them or quickly summarize enough from those lessons to make their points relevant here.

Show slide 9–15. Step 6: Evaluate or Test the Possible Choices.

This step continues the ***deductive*** part of the decision-making process.

Remind the learners that no option is ever perfect. Each option will have pros and cons. These pros and cons will be of different importance in the evaluation of the option. As decision makers, they will have to collect data on each option. How much information they need and where they get it will depend on what sort of decision they're making.

Return to the example of buying a car. Tell the class that the choices have been narrowed down to six possible choices. All fit the price, size, and four-wheel drive requirement set in step 3. Now they must gather and analyze further information on each of the options.

They will probably have several sources for this information. One source will be the cars themselves—doing test drives, kicking the tires, and smelling the upholstery. Another factor might be the salesperson. Still others would be publications such as *Consumer Reports* or similar magazines and websites that objectively evaluate automobiles. Other, possibly important, sources include their insurance agent, Uncle Harry, their spouse, and Joe (owner of Joe's Garage, who currently holds the mortgage to their house based on previous repair bills).

For a different sort of an example, let's say you're trying to hire a new employee. *Goal*: Hire an electrical engineer. *Limits*: $42,000 maximum salary; able to start work first of the month; must know about the industrial controls business. *Options*: You have received seven job applications.

Now you must evaluate these options (the applicants for the job). Undoubtedly, you'll find pros and cons to each prospective employee. To decide which applicant to hire, you'll have to collect more data on each and evaluate this data before you can make your decision. Later in the program, we will introduce a variety of tools and techniques to help you objectively review the list of options you've created and establish an objective, methodical means of evaluating each.

Note: If your program will not include modules 6 through 8, which cover methods for evaluating options, don't mention that aspect. Instead, edit slide 9–15 to remove the reference.

9:00 a.m. Break (10 minutes).

9:10 a.m. Step 7: Decide and Implement the Decision (10 minutes).

Show slide 9–16. The results of the evaluation in step 6 may lead to an obvious choice. On the other hand, there may be no obvious choice. Although some narrowing of the field of options and further data collection may help, the fact is, most decisions are calculated risks. The subject of risk is also covered in the next module.

The "best" decision may not be the cheapest. Lots of other considerations need to come into play, and they'll be discussed later in the training. For the moment, consider such things as the organizational culture, how big a change would be caused by your decision, how people might perceive things, and so on.

At this point you can implement the decision or recycle the decision-making process to a more specific level.

If the decision requires no further thought of great consequence, you can implement it. For example, if you've decided which engineering candidate you want to hire, do it. If you've decided which route to take from Cincinnati to Chicago, go for it. These decisions may be low-level enough that almost no further consideration is needed before you can put them into effect.

But perhaps you have a bigger goal: You want to start a business. In that case, maybe your limits in step 3 were the $50,000 you just inherited from Uncle Abner's will and your own job skills. Your options could have included opening up a shoe store, buying a pizza franchise, and starting a computer maintenance service. Your evaluation of these and other options included the potential profit for each, competition, legal issues, and so forth, and your choice was to open a shoe store.

Opening a shoe store is not a plan that can be implemented right away. It needs to be supplemented with a number of other, lower-level plans. This means you'll have to go back through the decision-making process several times. The decision of opening a shoe store has now become the new goal or objective for further decisions. You need to decide where to open the store. You need to decide how to advertise. You need to decide how to organize and staff the operation of the store. You need to decide how to obtain inventory. You may need to decide how to obtain further financing, and so forth.

So, you recycle through the decision-making process. A new, lower level, more specific, goal is to find a location for your shoe store. Limits would include geographic distribution of customers, costs of various locations (and whether to purchase or rent), and so forth. To determine your options, you call a commercial realtor or go through one or more of the processes in module 6. Your choice of a location may be a low-enough-level decision that you can just sign a lease to implement it. But you still have other specific plans to make about staff, inventory, additional financing, and so forth.

Note: Edit slide 9–16 to remove the last line if you will not be including module 9 in your program.

Show slide 9–17. Review of the Seven Steps.

Show slide 9–18. Thoughts About Decision Making. Read and discuss the quotes.

Show slide 9–19. Decision Making Isn't *All* Logic.

Discuss the points on the slide. Tell the class that they know the truth of these points intuitively.

Note that several bestselling books such as *Blink* by Malcolm Gladwell and *How We Decide* by Jonah Lehrer spell out the scientific research that proves those points.

Too much information can cause us to over-analyze things, and we are apt to make worse decisions. Several studies have shown that decision makers do much worse than random chance when faced with trying to decide why they chose one jelly over another (out of a couple of dozen choices). We become overwhelmed and lose perspective.

The more complex a problem, the less we can rely on simple rationality. Even so, the process suggested earlier (and continued throughout this training) will help structure things into more manageable elements.

Golfers, tennis players, chess players, and experts in almost any area can ruin their game by thinking too much. Once you are an expert in something, you have developed subconscious and innate skills, and you need to trust them.

9:20 a.m. Application Exercise (30 minutes).

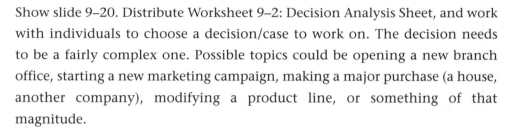

Show slide 9–20. Distribute Worksheet 9–2: Decision Analysis Sheet, and work with individuals to choose a decision/case to work on. The decision needs to be a fairly complex one. Possible topics could be opening a new branch office, starting a new marketing campaign, making a major purchase (a house, another company), modifying a product line, or something of that magnitude.

Note: Work with people to choose something appropriate as they begin this training. If they're trying to choose which tie to wear to the fund raiser next week, they will not be able to apply the learning very effectively.

9:50 a.m. Module 1 Summary (10 minutes).

Show slide 9–21. Review the objectives covered in this module. At this point, you may want to preview the next module and announce any work to be done ahead of time.

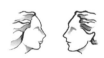

LEARNING CHECK QUESTIONS

You can use the learning check questions and answers in oral or printed form.

Discussion Questions

♦   Give examples of *limits* as the term applies to the decision-making process.

   Answer: time, money, space, people, equipment, technology, and so forth.

♦   Why is it important to separate step 4 and step 5 in the decision-making process?

   Answer: They use different sides of the brain; flip-flopping wastes time and can encourage adopting the first workable answer, and so forth.

◆ What is meant by *recycle* as one of the possible options in the last step of decision making?

Answer: Some decisions are small enough to implement without exhaustive research, but others provide the foundation for further decision making. For the latter, you need to recycle the decision-making process at a lower level.

◆ Name three reasons why it's important to understand the structure of the decision-making process.

Answer: It can (1) give the decision maker confidence, (2) provide a proven process, and (3) assist in gathering and developing necessary information in the most efficient manner.

◆ List the steps in decision making.

Answer: Step 1: Determine That a Decision Is Needed

Step 2: Determine the Importance of the Decision

Step 3: Assess What Limits Apply to the Decision

Step 4: Determine Possible Choices

Step 5: Gather Information About the Choices

Step 6: Evaluate or Test the Possible Choices

Step 7: Decide and Implement the Decision

◆ What are the potential problems (if any) with a decision being made the "wrong" way, as long as it results in an acceptable outcome?

Answer: Possible inefficiencies, including backtracking, false starts, and so forth. By doing it the "proper" way, you have a predictable pattern, you can develop documentation as you go along, and you can retrace your steps. Moreover, a well-defined process is generally likely to be more efficient and effective.

Multiple Choice Questions

1. Which of the following is *not* directly related to a decision's importance?

   a. The amount of information is available to help make it *(answer)*.

    b. Who is involved with it?

    c. Can the decision be changed later?

    d. How much does the decision cost in comparison to budget?

2. Before facts relevant to the various alternatives can be gathered, one must first

    a. Identify possible alternatives

    b. Identify the problem

    c. Select the best alternative

    d. Both a and b *(answer)*

10:00 a.m. Thank You for Your Attention.

Show slide 9–22. Edit this slide to include information relevant to your class.

Worksheet 9–1
Icebreaker

Icebreaker Instructions:

Pair off with someone you don't know well.

You have three minutes each to exchange answers to the following questions.

Name?

_____

_____

_____

How long have you been with the organization?

_____

_____

_____

What's your job title?

_____

_____

_____

What's the most recent significant decision you've had to make for the organization?

_____

_____

_____

What hobby or family obligation (that you're willing to share) takes up your time away from the job?

_____

_____

_____

When the trainer gathers the group back together, you will be asked to take one minute or less to introduce your companion to the rest of the group.

Worksheet 9–2

Decision Analysis Sheet

In one sentence or less, specify the decision you need to make:

_____

Is this decision necessary?

* What will happen if no decision is made? _____
* Are there advantages to not making the decision? _____
* What are the disadvantages? _____
* Do you have the authority and power to make and implement the decision? _____
  If not, why are you involved? _____
* Could someone else make this decision better than you? _____
  Who? _____ Why don't they? _____

How important is the decision?

* How much is the probable cost? _____
  How does that compare to your total budget? _____
* How long is the commitment? _____
* Can it be changed later? _____
  How expensive or messy would a later change be? _____
* How soon does the decision have to be made? _____
* Who else is involved? _____

What limits apply to this decision?

* List all major factors that will affect or be affected by this decision:
  People _____
  Equipment _____
  Facilities _____
  Time _____
  Competition _____
  Management skills _____
  The economy _____
  Budget, now and future _____
  Others _____

Evaluation Instrument 9-1
Pretest on Decision Making

Circle either true or false:

T	F	1. We all make hundreds of decisions every day.
T	F	2. All decisions are made in an essentially similar pattern.
T	F	3. Choices should be evaluated as they appear.
T	F	4. Decision making applies to all phases of management or supervision.
T	F	5. Creativity is not necessary in *most* decision making.
T	F	6. Intuition is more important than rational thought in the early stages of decision making.
T	F	7. Limits should be established early in the decision-making process.
T	F	8. Tolerance for risk influences decision making for managers.
T	F	9. Good decisions are both properly made and effective.
T	F	10. Organizational decisions tend to be more "convoluted" than "straightforward" in nature.

List several decisions that you either have made in the past couple of weeks or you will need to make in the next several weeks. These will serve as the basis for discussion during this program.

MAKING EFFECTIVE DECISIONS

Module 1
The Anatomy of a Decision

Slide 9–1

Today's Agenda

- Introductions
- Overview of the Program
- Pretest and Discussion
- The Process of Making a Decision
- Application
- Wrap-Up and Preview

Slide 9–2

Pretest

Complete the handout.
You'll have five minutes, so don't over-analyze the questions.

Slide 9–3

Thoughts About Decision Making

- "More than any time in history, mankind faces a crossroads. One path leads to despair and utter hopelessness, the other to total extinction. Let us pray that we have the wisdom to choose correctly."

— Woody Allen

Slide 9–4

Answers to the Pretest

1. True
2. True
3. False
4. True
5. True (most decisions are programmed or routine)
6. True
7. True (but only "limited" limits)
8. True
9. True
10. True

Slide 9–5

Module 1 Topics

After completing this module, you should be able to:

- List and explain the steps by which a decision is made
- Explain the benefits of a structured decision-making process
- Determine the relative importance of a decision.

Slide 9–6

Why Is a Process Important?

- **First**, it can give us confidence that we can handle the situation.
- **Second**, it can provide a discipline to follow as we work through the process.
- **Finally**, it can allow us to concurrently develop the information and support necessary to get others to buy into the idea.

Slide 9–7

Thoughts About Decision Making

- "Start with the end in mind."

 — Steven Covey

Slide 9–8

Steps in Decision Making

1. Determine that a decision is needed.
2. Determine the decision's importance.
3. Assess what limits apply to the decision.
4. Determine possible choices.
5. Gather information about the possible choices.
6. Evaluate or test the possible choices.
7. Decide and implement the decision (or recycle).

Slide 9–9

Step 1. Determine That a Decision Is Needed

- Does it have to be decided?
- Do I have the authority or power to make and implement the decision?
- Do I have or can I get the necessary information to make the decision?
- Who else could make it better?

Slide 9–10

Step 2: Determine the Decision's Importance

- How much does it cost?
- How long is the commitment?
- Who is involved?
- Can it be changed later?
- How soon does it have to be made?
- How much information is available to make the decision?

Slide 9–11

Step 3: Assess What Limits Apply to the Decision

Limits have to do with available resources:

- Time
- Money
- Equipment or facilities
- Technological capabilities
- People
- Technical and managerial skills
- Other resources
- Etc. What will affect progress toward the goal?

Slide 9–12

Step 4: Determine Possible Choices

- Complete step 4 before you even consider step 5.
- You almost never need to consider *all* options.
- Techniques and tools will be covered in modules 2 through 5.

Slide 9–13

Step 5: Gather Information About the Choices

- Too much information can be as bad as too little information.
- Limit your choices and collect data selectively.

Slide 9–14

Step 6: Evaluate or Test the Possible Choices

- Can be done in many ways; it all depends on the nature of the decision.
- Tools and techniques will be discussed in modules 6–8.

Slide 9–15

Step 7: Decide and Implement the Decision (or "Recycle")

- The best decision is not always the cheapest or most easily implemented.
- Many other factors must be considered:
  - Organizational culture
  - People's needs and tolerance for change
  - Perception
- More on this in module 9.

Slide 9–16

Review of Seven Steps

1. Determine that a decision is needed.
2. Determine the decision's importance.
3. Assess what limits apply to the decision.
4. Determine possible choices.
5. Gather information about the possible choices.
6. Evaluate or test the possible choices.
7. Decide and implement the decision/recycle.

Slide 9–17

Thoughts About Decision Making

- Truly successful decision making relies on a balance between deliberate and instinctive thinking.
  —Malcolm Gladwell
- Rationality can lead us astray; we focus on too much to manage.
  —Jonah Lehrer

Slide 9–18

Decision Making Isn't *All* Logic

- There's often too much to analyze.
- Simple problems require reason, but complicated problems also require emotions.
- A balance is needed between deliberate and instinctive thinking.

Slide 9–19

Application Exercise

- Choose one (or two) of the decisions you listed at the end of your pretest.
- Complete the handout questionnaire
- Discuss your handout with a classmate
- Choose a fairly broad decision, as you will be asked to continue working on it throughout this training program.

Slide 9–20

Module 1 Summary

1. Name three reasons why it's important to understand the structure of the decision-making process.
2. List the seven steps in decision making.
3. How do you determine the importance of a decision?

Slide 9–21

Thank You for Your Attention

- Next meeting:
- Assignment:
- Other announcements?

Slide 9–22

Module 2—The Creative Process: Developing Options

Module 2 is recommended for all decision-making programs—half-day, full-day, and two-day—except for half-day programs for managers and supervisors, which use only modules 1 and 9. Module 2 introduces the subjects of creativity and risk in decision making.

Training Objectives

After completing module 2, the participants should be able to

- explain the importance of creativity in decision making
- clarify the goal of a decision
- develop or identify viable options from which to choose
- calculate the degree of risk related to a decision.

Module 2 Time

- Approximately 1 hour

Introduction, welcome, and review	5 minutes
PowerPoint presentation	30 minutes
Worksheet exercise and discussion	20 minutes
Wrap-up, learning check, and preview	5 minutes

Note: This includes time for a quick review at the start and a learning check at the end.

Materials

- Attendance list
- Pencils, pens, and paper for each participant

- ◆ Whiteboard or flipchart and markers

- ◆ Name tags or name tents for each participant

- ◆ Worksheet 10–1: Decision Analysis Sheet

- ◆ Computer, screen, and projector for displaying PowerPoint slides; alternatively, overhead projector and overhead transparencies

- ◆ PowerPoint slide program (slides 10–1 through 10–14)

- ◆ This chapter for reference or detailed facilitator notes

- ◆ Optional: music, coffee or other refreshments.

Module Preparation

Arrive ahead of time to greet the participants and make sure materials are available and laid out appropriately for the way you want to run the class.

Sample Agenda

0:00   Welcome class.

Have slide 10–1 up on the screen as participants arrive; go to slide 10–2 as you begin.

Preview the agenda (the objectives) for this session. Ask for questions or concerns.

Use slide 10–3 to review the previous module.

0:05   PPT Presentation.

Begin with slide 10–4 and proceed through slide 10–10.

0:35   Worksheets.

Distribute Worksheet 10–1 (Decision Analysis Sheet)

Show slide 10–11 as the participants work on the worksheet. Show slide 10–12 as work continues.

Move among participants to keep them on task.

Have participants discuss the answers with others.

0:55   Wrap-up.

Use slide 10–13 to review the objectives with participants.

Ask for questions from participants.

Check learning—questions can be oral or printed (see below).

Show slide 10–14. Dismiss the class.

Trainer's Notes

8:00 a.m. Welcome participants (5 minutes).

Show slide 10–1 as participants arrive.

Take care of housekeeping items.

8:05 a.m. Creativity in Decision Making (10 minutes).

Show slide 10–2 and preview the module topics.

Show slide 10–3 and briefly review module 1.

Depending on how long it has been since the module was presented, you may skip this step. If you do use slide 10–3, you can say that module 1 covered seven steps in the decision-making process. This session will focus on Step 4, developing lists of options from which to choose. This is the "inductive" or creative part of decision making, also thought of as the "right brain" part, because that's where it happens.

Show slide 10–4. Say the word *creating*. Note that the word implies some higher power. It is the process by which new or different things and ideas develop. Creating is something that most of us feel inadequately prepared to do. We don't have that higher power, that extra skill, that unique insight that allows us to exclaim "aha!" as a light bulb magically appears above our heads.

Or do we? Look around at the people society considers creative: artists, advertising writers, inventors, journalists, and others.

Thomas Edison was much admired for his dogged determination in the face of thousands of failures to reach his few, albeit important successes. He even claimed that, "Success is 1 percent inspiration and 99 percent perspiration."

Can you and I learn to be creative? Many books and articles on the subject are available, but the short answer is "Yes." People are creative either because they have learned to be or because they somehow avoided developing or being hampered by blocks to creativity, some of which society presents to us. Note that the next module will deal with overcoming the blocks that get in the way of creativity.

Show slide 10–5.

If you think about it, you are already creative. Creativity does not require artistic talent or great skill or even above-average intelligence.

Think about your dreams. They are usually unstructured. Much of the time our creativity is unstructured, but, oddly enough, bringing in structure can help us to increase the creativity.

In terms of decision making, the first thing that must happen is to clarify what is expected from the decision.

8:15 a.m. The Goal of the Decision (10 minutes).

Show slide 10–6. Regardless of the specifics, what we're dealing with here is a relatively simple idea: *What do you want to happen?* You must define the desired outcome of a decision before you can build a plan to make it happen. A cliché about decision making warns us: "If you don't know where you're going, you'll never know if you've arrived." Therefore, an important part of decision making is to establish your goals.

We usually get into making a decision because we either have an opportunity or a problem. If it's a problem, the way we know that the problem exists is that we see its *effects*.

Note: Insert an example here, preferably a real-life example involving the organization itself.

At this stage in the decision-making process, you should put down *in writing* the related information you see as "facts." Putting the facts on paper helps to clarify your understanding of the problem or opportunity. The facts need to be in writing to keep them clear and specific in the decision makers' minds. Otherwise, the issue may become something of an "amorphous blob."

Frequently, we may find that what we thought were accurate "facts" change as we get more information on the issue. Yes, that does mean the facts were probably wrong in the original assessment. Don't waste time justifying why the facts changed; just move on. Simply restate the "facts" to reflect the new information. After all, if the complete information had been available in the first place, most likely there would be no problem to solve or decision to make.

A good way to handle this step of the decision-making process is to make several short lists. Two of these lists should be "facts" about:

1. What *is* true regarding the situation at this point?

2. What is *not* true regarding the situation at this point?

You may need some other lists, too. For example, let's say the decision is what to do about standards not being met. In that case, another list should specify these facts. For example:

If standards were being met before, what changed? Listing facts is important because we often mistake one issue for another or believe that symptoms are really causes. Listing facts is an essential prelude to identifying the real goal.

Because the top goal isn't always obvious, the manager may have to make several tries before being able to state what the goal really is.

Using cause-and-effect logic will help here (we'll cover that in detail in module 5). But we usually start with the effect, that is, what's *not* happening that *should be* happening (or vice versa). The effect (the deviation from what we want) is the problem that we must solve.

So, after listing the facts, we must test reality: If any of the facts or answers to questions are inconsistent with the undesirable effect (the deviation or issue at hand), then either we don't have the *real* issue defined yet or the "fact" is wrong. To find out where we went wrong, we have to backtrack to the root cause of this effect and see if it is the issue. We have to keep looking for a prior, more basic, issue that, if resolved, will eliminate the current undesirable effect.

Once the goal—eliminating the root cause of the problem—is determined, move on to developing your choices for solving the problem.

8:25 a.m. The Difference Between Cause and Effect (5 minutes).

Show slide 10–7. How can a person not understand the issue? Let's say a manager is quite concerned that the work in his or her area is not being accomplished. The manager may know for a fact that high absenteeism exists in the department. From that fact, he or she has decided that high absenteeism is the cause of the problem. However, absenteeism may only be a *symptom* of other, deeper issues.

People may be absent because they know there aren't enough parts to do the job, and that if they come to work they'll just sit around or be sent home. Or they may be absent because the area is so dusty that they're getting sick. In either case, the absenteeism isn't the cause, it's only a symptom of a larger issue.

If the managers start out with the wrong assumption, they'll have to back-track to find the real issue. They should list "high absenteeism" as a fact, nothing more. When they begin to determine the available options, it will be important to know about the absenteeism, but some other facts will also be needed. *Note:* Insert a real-life example here.

8:30 a.m. Developing Choices (5 minutes).

Show slide 10–8. Because this slide was part of the previous module, discuss it here only as a refresher. Remember the basics about developing your choices: Always consider *all* options before you gather information about them, and realize that you will never be able to consider every possible option.

How many options are enough? It depends on the nature of the decision. We'll look closely at this issue later in the program and develop a variety of ways to create a broader and more effective list of options. For now, though, let's say that four to 12 options are adequate for most decisions.

Show slide 10–9: Where to Get Ideas. Ideas are all around you; they come from other people, your own imagination and dreams, books you read, catalogs, movies, the Internet, nature, things that happen to you, and so on. Where you find them, of course, depends on what kind of a decision you're trying to make. Module 5 in this training will suggest a number of techniques for improving your creativity. For now, however, we'll move on to consider the amount of risk people are willing to take as they make decisions.

8:35 a.m. Risk in Decisions (5 minutes).

Show slide 10–10. This is an introduction to the part risk plays in decision making. If you are delivering all of the training modules, you will cover risk more fully in module 7.

We know from personal experience and observing others that people vary in the amount of risk they will take. We will leave to the behavioral scientists the reasons behind the phenomenon of risk taking. But we do know that decision making is influenced by such things as personality, the consequences of loss, the benefits of gain, group pressure, and many other things, even including the way in which the risk is stated.

Some people, called **risk averters** will take lower risks than indicated by the probabilities, whereas others, called **gamblers** will take greater risks. It might seem logical that if a person is given a decision with a 75 percent probability of one choice being the correct one, it would be chosen. This is not necessarily true, however, because there is a 25 percent chance of the decision being wrong. Some people will avoid even small risks, especially if the penalty for being wrong is severe.

As shown by the darker line in the graph on slide 10–10, most people will take some risk when the commitment is low, but will become conservative as the stakes increase. You might be willing to bet $1 at 10:1 to win a payoff of $5. When it's a $100 bet for $500 at the same odds, though, most of us are more reluctant. It's not the *odds* (they're both 10 to one against you) or the *payoff* (both are five to one if you win), but the *size of the commitment.* We can afford to lose the $1, but not the $100.

Probability (shown on the vertical axis of the chart) is an important concept in the analysis of risk. We all hear weather reports saying that the "probability of rain is 60 percent." What does this really mean? Does it mean that of the five meteorologists in the office, three think it will rain? Maybe.

The higher the risk, then, the more information we will probably want to collect to help ensure that our decision is correct.

Formulas exist in management science that can help determine the value of additional information. A simplified way of dealing with the question of how much information you'll try to obtain is to ask, "What will be the cost of additional information (in time, money, or other resources)?" And to also ask, "What is the risk of deciding without it?" Sometimes those answers can be quantified, but often they can't. So, seeking more information becomes a judgment call. If the risk is low and the additional information is expensive or time consuming to obtain, odds are that it won't be worth it. If the risk is high and the additional information can be obtained easily, then go ahead and get it.

Remember, research into this issue shows that the threat of losses has a more significant effect on decisions than the expectation of gains.

8:40 a.m. Thoughts About Decision Making (15 minutes).

Show slide 10–11. Distribute Worksheet 10–1 (Decision Analysis Sheet).

The question is: Do you think the person described in the slide is a risk averter?

Allow participants time to work on the worksheet.

Show slide 10–12. Ask participants to discuss the answers with each other.

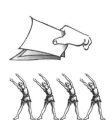

8:55 a.m. Module 2 Summary (5 minutes).

Show slide 10–13. Review the module 2 objectives with participants and ask for questions. Use the learning check questions below to finish the class.

LEARNING CHECK QUESTIONS

You can use the learning check questions and answers in oral or printed form.

Discussion Question

◆ What influences the amount of risk an individual will take when making a decision?

Answer: It's complicated, but it starts with the individual's personality and is adjusted by the importance of the decision and the consequences of being wrong.

Multiple Choice Questions

1. Creativity is

    a. Directly related to intelligence

    b. Directly related to artistic ability

    c. Requires a great amount of skill and practice

    d. All of the above *(answer)*

    e. None of the above

2. Creativity is

    a. A natural activity in most children

    b. Often limited by society and culture

    c. Generally associated with the right side of the brain

    d. All of the above *(answer)*

    e. None of the above

3. People vary in their tolerance of risk. Someone who is unlikely to bet, even on a nearly sure thing, would be called a

   a. Right-brained thinker

   b. Risk averter *(answer)*

   c. Gambler

   d. Left-brained thinker

9:00 a.m. Thank You for Your Attention.

Show slide 10–14. Edit this slide to include appropriate information about your class. Dismiss the class.

Worksheet 10–1
Decision Analysis Sheet

Restate the decision(s) you were working with in the previous module.

_____

What do you want to happen as a result of the decision? (Be specific.)

_____

What do you know to be true about the situation?

_____

What do you know to be not true?

_____

What has changed, if anything?

_____

Information Required

List *at least* four things you need or want to know to be able to make this decision:

◆ _____ ( )

◆ _____ ( )

◆ _____ ( )

◆ _____ ( )

◆ _____ ( )

◆ _____ ( )

In the parentheses, order them by importance to the quality of the decision.
How much risk is involved in this decision, and how did you determine that?

_____

MAKING EFFECTIVE DECISIONS

Module 2
The Creative Process:
Developing Options

Slide 10–1

Module 2 Topics

- Explain the importance of creativity in decision making.
- Clarify the goal of a decision.
- Develop or identify viable options from which to choose.
- Calculate the degree of risk related to a decision.

Slide 10–2

Review: Decision-Making Steps

1. Determine that a decision is needed.
2. Determine the decision's importance.
3. Assess what limits apply to the decision.
4. **Determine possible choices.**
5. Gather information about the possible choices.
6. Evaluate or test the possible choices.
7. Decide and implement the decision (or recycle).

Slide 10–3

Creativity Is Important

Slide 10–4

You Already Are Creative

- You dream nearly every night.
- You solve problems.
- You may also have artistic talents, etc.

But...

- Being creative does not require being artistic.
- Being creative does not demand great skill.
- Being creative is not a function of intelligence.

Slide 10–5

Clarifying the Goal of the Decision

- Specify what you want to happen as a result of the decision making process.
- Write down related facts about the issue.
  - What is true about the situation
  - What is not true
  - What has changed
  - What is not known that we need to find out.

Slide 10–6

Separate Cause From Effect

Slide 10–7

Developing Choices

- Complete step 4 before you even consider step 5.
- You almost never need to consider *all* options.
- An "adequate" list of options may be a couple up to a dozen.

Slide 10–8

Where to Get Ideas

Slide 10–9

Risk in Decisions

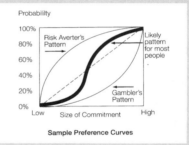

Slide 10–10

Thoughts About Decision Making

- I knew a man who had so much trouble making decisions, that when he was asked his favorite color, he always said, "Plaid."
  — Anonymous

Slide 10–11

Application Exercise

- Refine the decision(s) you are working on using the instructions on the worksheet.
- Discuss your answers with your group.

Slide 10–12

Module 2 Summary

- Explain the importance of creativity in decision making.
- Clarify the goal of a decision.
- Develop or identify viable options from which to choose.
- Calculate the degree of risk related to a decision.

Slide 10–13

Thank You for Your Attention

- Next meeting:
- Assignment:
- Other announcements?

Slide 10–14

♦

Module 3—Barriers to Creativity

This module elaborates on the subject of the barriers to creativity. Use it in any program that lasts more than one day.

Training Objectives

After completing this module, the participants should be able to identify

- six kinds of barriers that may affect decision making

- personal traits related to decision making

- group traits related to decision making.

Module 3 Time

- Approximately 1 hour

Introduction, welcome, and review of previous module	5 minutes
PowerPoint presentation	25 minutes
Worksheet exercise	15 minutes
Group discussion of barriers	10 minutes
Wrap-up, learning check, optional worksheet, and preview	5 minutes

Note: This includes time for a quick review at the start and a learning check at the end.

Materials

- Attendance list

- Pencils, pens, and paper for each participant

- ◆ Whiteboard or flipchart and markers

- ◆ Name tags or name tents for each participant

- ◆ Worksheet 11–1: Creative Barriers

- ◆ Worksheet 11–2: Word Puzzles (optional)

- ◆ Computer, screen, and projector for displaying PowerPoint slides; alternatively, overhead projector and overhead transparencies

- ◆ PowerPoint slide program (slides 11–1 through 11–12)

- ◆ This chapter for reference or detailed facilitator notes

- ◆ Optional: music, coffee or other refreshments, selection of puzzles, and brainteasers.

Module Preparation

Arrive ahead of time to greet the participants and make sure materials are available and laid out for the way you want to run the class.

Sample Agenda

0:00 Welcome the class.

Have slide 11–1 up on the screen as people arrive; go to slide 11–2 as you begin.

Preview the agenda for this session (the objectives).

Ask for questions or concerns.

0:05 PPT Presentation.

Begin with slide 11–3; pause for discussion, then proceed through slide 11–8.

0:30 Worksheets.

Distribute Worksheet 11–1: Creative Barriers.

Show slide 11–9 as participants work on the worksheet.

Move among participants to keep them on task.

Have participants discuss answers with others.

0:50   Group discussion.

Show slide 11–10 and hold a discussion about the barriers that participants identified earlier in the session and on their worksheets.

0:55   Wrap-up.

Show slide 11–11. Review the objectives with participants.

Ask for questions.

Check learning (questions can be oral or printed—see below).

Introduce optional Worksheet 11–2: Word Puzzles.

Show slide 11–12. Dismiss the class.

Trainer's Notes

8:00 a.m. Welcome (5 minutes).

Show slide 11–1 as participants arrive.

Take care of housekeeping items.

8:05 a.m. Preview the Module Topics (5 minutes).

Show slide 11–2, which provides a preview of the module. Show slide 11–3. Review quotes from *Alice in Wonderland*.

8:10 a.m. Creativity Barriers (20 minutes).

Show slide 11–4.

Perhaps it was in kindergarten, or certainly by first grade, that you learned that society doesn't always appreciate creativity. We are taught that we must—to a point—limit our natural childlike tendencies to do things our own way. Although suppressing our urge to do things our own way can be taught in ways that don't unnecessarily inhibit creativity, the usual pattern is to encourage conformity.

"Color within the lines, Johnny." "No, Sally, frogs are not red and blue; they're green." "If any of you have to go to the bathroom, raise your hand." (I always wondered how that would help.) As we get older, we face more and more rules:

"Drive on the right side of the road." "Work starts at 8:00 a.m." Some rules (such as the one about driving) are obviously necessary for safety or for the functioning of society in an orderly way. Others, however, are not.

The most insidious barriers to creativity are those unnecessary blocks we place on ourselves for a variety of reasons.

Get participants to add their own ideas to the list of barriers to creativity. If the class and company culture permits, you can discuss the creativity barriers that participants encounter in their own workplace. The Dilbert cartoons by Scott Adams usually come up. Keep this process somewhat in check so you don't go over the scheduled time. Tell people that the main idea here is not to "vent," but to take these barriers and apply them to James L. Adams' model. (Adams' 1974 book *Conceptual Blockbusting* is the foundation for this list. Although trained as an engineer, Adams became best known for his work in creativity, and he was also a key scientist involved with several NASA missions.)

Also, let participants know that the next module will discuss ways to overcome these barriers.

Show slide 11–5. Go over the six types of barriers to creativity: emotional, environmental, perceptual, intellectual, cultural, and expressive. Then, show slide 11–6.

Emotional Blocks: Examples of emotional blocks include fear, need for security, preference for judging, impatience, and more. An individual who chooses to not try out a new concept may have an emotional block to the concept.

Environmental Blocks: Examples include distractions such as the telephone, email, and chatty colleagues; lack of cooperation from co-workers; autocratic bosses; bureaucracy; things in the workplace that keep you from being creative; and so on. Provide your own examples and ask for examples from the learners.

Work environments are filled with environmental blocks. No single technique works to overcome these, but time management techniques can sometimes reduce them.

Show slide 11–7.

Perceptual Blocks: Mistakes in perceptions include seeing what we expect to see (instead of what's really there) and not being able to view things differently or from another perspective. Perceptual blocks prevent us from clearly perceiving either the problem itself or accurately seeing information necessary to solve the problem. Too many people spend inadequate time defining the problem. They're impatient to get on with the "important" part—solving the problem. This can result in a "ready, shoot, aim" tendency.

Take, for example, the manager who has decided that the maintenance department is inept but in reality is blind to the real problem, which is that the equipment is beyond repair.

Intellectual Blocks: Sometimes we simply don't understand the concepts needed to work on the problem. If you don't have the experience, academic training, or mental abilities sophisticated enough to understand and deal with the issues surrounding the problem or decision, it's difficult to be creative. It could also be that you're locked into a bad approach. Managers who have been promoted from the ranks of workers often find themselves falling behind technologically, especially in fast-changing fields. Their subordinates may understand new and advanced techniques that would work, but the manager may resist using them, fearing loss of control.

Show slide 11–8.

Cultural Blocks: These blocks include taboos; traditions; excessive belief in logic, reason, and numbers; or distrust of fantasy or intuition.

In short, behaving the way we're "supposed to" means conforming to the normal way of doing things—the opposite of thinking creatively. As will be discussed later in the program, each organization has a unique culture. Conforming to that culture at most times may be essential to getting along in organization, but conforming may also inhibit the implementation of changes that would improve the organization.

Expressive Blocks: Another barrier to creativity arises when a person has inadequate language skill to express and record ideas so he or she can be understood by others. This applies not only to language barriers but also to using the wrong or inappropriate medium to express concepts, such as trying to express a visual idea orally or a mathematical idea in visual terms.

In today's diverse workplace, managers may find themselves with subordinates and peers who—literally—speak different languages. It takes so much energy for routine communications in these environments that creativity may be reduced.

8:30 a.m. Creative Barriers Worksheet (20 minutes).

Distribute Worksheet 11–1: Creativity Barriers.

Show slide 11–9 as the attendees work on the worksheet. Review the instructions on the PowerPoint slide and on the actual worksheet. Then proceed with the exercise.

INSTRUCTIONS FOR WORKSHEET 11–1: BARRIERS TO CREATIVITY

Objective of the worksheet: This is the third in a series of worksheets. It incorporates one or two topics that were identified in the pretest by participants as decisions they would soon need to make. Each participant will work throughout all the sessions (up to 10, depending on the length of the program) on their personally chosen topics. If the same topic has been chosen by a group, rather than an individual, the worksheet can be completed by one person for the group based on their discussion of the questions.

Time required: Allow approximately 20 minutes for participants to answer the questions.

Instructor guidance: The questions on the worksheet refer to points that were covered in the module 3 presentation, and a summary is included in each box as a memory tool. Walk among the participants during the 20 minutes allowed and try to keep them on task. If some participants finish early, encourage them to work with someone else who is having a problem coming up with answers to write down. If some are not finished by the end of the time, have them continue to think about it and complete the worksheet before the next meeting. Session 4 will build on the answers the participants have recorded on this worksheet.

Wrap-up: At the end of the allotted time, ask the participants to keep the worksheets and bring back for the next session. Return to show the final PowerPoint slide for the module, and ask review questions before dismissing the participants.

8:50 a.m. Traits That Influence Decisions (5 minutes).

Show slide 11–10. Discuss the questions on the PowerPoint slide as a group.

8:55 a.m. Module 3 Summary (5 minutes).

Show slide 11–11. The last two items on this slide were implied in the discussion, and may have come up based on the discussion of the previous slide. Just in case they didn't, a couple of individual traits would be (1) tolerance for ambiguity and (2) skill in dealing with data (such as statistics). There are many others.

Group traits would include the norms (traditions and informal rules) established by the group, lack of a different perspective, and so on.

LEARNING CHECK QUESTIONS

You can use the learning check questions and answers in oral or printed form.

Discussion Questions

- ◆ What are the six types of barriers to creativity?

  Answer: emotional, environmental, perceptual, intellectual, cultural, and expressive.

- ◆ Pick any two of types of blocks, and give an example of how each might affect your decision-making process in selecting a movie to attend. What would you do to guard against these barriers to effective decisions?

  Answers will vary from participant to participant.

Multiple Choice Question

1. The fear of making a mistake is an example of a _____ barrier.

   a. Emotional *(answer)*

   b. Perceptual

   c. Intellectual

   d. Environmental

Instructions for Worksheet 11–2: Word Puzzles (Optional Exercise)

Optional exercise: Add 15 minutes.

Objective of this worksheet: Although this worksheet adds some fun to the training session, its real purpose is to demonstrate how the mind causes several of the barriers to creativity that were discussed in the program.

Time required: Allow about five minutes for people to come up with the answers. More than that will frustrate the participants and, unless they've seen these before, almost no one ever gets 100 percent of the answers. It will take less than two minutes to give the answers and tie them back to the examples in the session.

Instructor guidance: The answers are included with the worksheet. Do not print that part of the sheet. People may work in groups, if you've been doing that, or individually. You might have a small prize for the person who can correctly identify the largest number of anagrams. Be sure to explain at least several of the examples cited in the answer section so that participants can understand the purpose of the exercise and tie it back to the content of the module.

Move among the participants to keep them on task. Discuss with the participants the barriers covered earlier in the class.

Use Worksheet 11–2: Word Puzzles as an optional creative exercise. You can find puzzles like this in a variety of places, from *The Reader's Digest* to Internet sites. They're fun and can be educational (what barriers were responsible for your inability to see the answer right away?), but be aware that the session may extend beyond the budgeted one hour if you go through more than just a few brainteasers.

9:00 a.m. Thank You for Your Attention.

Show slide 11–12. Edit this slide to include information relevant to your class.

Worksheet 11–1
Creativity Barriers

Restate the decision you're working on:

_____

What are some possible barriers that may prevent you from coming up with options for your sample decision? Mark those that relate to a group and those that relate to an individual.

Emotional. Examples: fear of making mistakes, failing, or taking risks; need for security, order, and structure; preference for judging rather than generating ideas; impatience
Environmental. Examples: distractions such as the telephone, emails, and chatty colleagues; lack of cooperation from co-workers; autocratic bosses; bureaucracy
Perceptual. Examples: seeing what we expect to see, not being able to view things differently, spending inadequate time defining the problem to get on with the "important" part of solving it

continued on next page

Worksheet 11–1, continued

Creativity Barriers

Intellectual. Examples: inexperience, lack of academic training or mental abilities sophisticated enough to understand and deal with the issues surrounding the problem or decision, being locked into a bad approach

Cultural. Examples: taboos, traditions, excessive belief in logic, reason, numbers; distrust of fantasy, intuition, and different drummers; in short, behaving the way we're "supposed to" is conforming, not creative

Expressive. Examples: inadequate language skill to express and record ideas in a manner that can be understood by others, or using the wrong or inappropriate medium to express concepts, such as trying to express a visual idea orally or a mathematical idea in visual terms

Notes:

Worksheet 11–2
Word Puzzles

Each of the following squares contains a word puzzle that can be read as a common phrase or saying. How many of them can you get? Which barriers to creativity may be operating to keep you from seeing them at first?

MAN BOARD	STAND I	CA SE CASE
$\dfrac{\text{KNEE}}{\text{LIGHT}}$	LE VEL	$\dfrac{0}{\begin{array}{c}\text{M.D.}\\\text{B.A.}\\\text{PH.D.}\end{array}}$
| | 0 0 0 0 0 0	 TRAP	ECNALG
CLOUDY	MOMANON	$\underline{\text{READING}}$
LATE N_eV_er	NITNIT	◯ ME

continued on next page

Worksheet 11–2, continued
Word Puzzles

Answers:

First row: Man Overboard

I Understand (Most people start out trying "stand on I" or "stand on 1." They use what worked in the first box.)

Open and shut case

Second row: Neon light (This is different from the first two boxes because it requires conjoining the first word and the preposition to make a different word. Again, the pattern that worked before must be altered.)

Split level (or bi-level)

Three degrees below zero

Third row: Circles under the eyes

Mouse trap

Backwards glance

Fourth row: Partly (or mostly) cloudy

Man in the moon

Reading between the lines

Fifth row: Better late than never

Bottom half of the ninth

A round on me (which you might be ready for by now)

MAKING EFFECTIVE DECISIONS

Module 3
Barriers to Creativity

Slide 11–1

Module 3 Topics

- Identify six kinds of barriers to effective decision making.
- Identify personal traits related to decision making.
- Identify group traits related to decision making.

Slide 11–2

Thoughts About Decision Making

" Cheshire Puss, would you tell me, please, which way I ought to walk from here?"

"That depends a good deal on where you want to get to," said the Cat.

"I don't much care where…" said Alice.

"Then it doesn't matter which way you walk," said the Cat.

"…so long as I get somewhere," Alice added as an explanation.

"Oh, you're sure to do that," said the Cat, "if only you walk long enough."

— Lewis Carroll

Slide 11–3

Creativity Barriers

Some of the Rules From Kindergarten

"Color within the lines, Johnny."
"No, Sally, frogs are not red and blue; they're green."
"If any of you have to go to the bathroom, raise your hand."

As we get older, we face more and more rules:

"Drive on the right side of the road."
"Work starts at 8:00 a.m."

Slide 11–4

Six Barriers to Creativity

J. L. Adams

- Emotional
- Environmental
- Perceptual
- Intellectual
- Cultural
- Expressive

Slide 11–5

Examples of Barriers

- Emotional:
  - Fear of making mistakes or failing
  - Impatience
  - Preference for judging rather than creating
  - Too much need for order or security
  - Etc.
- Environmental:
  - Noise
  - Phone calls
  - Autocratic bosses
  - Bureaucracy
  - Lack of cooperation
  - Etc.

Slide 11–6

Examples of Barriers (continued)

- Perceptual:
  - Seeing what you expect to see
  - Lack of a different perspective or point of view
  - Etc.
- Intellectual:
  - Lack of experience in the area being discussed
  - Lack of education or training
  - Lack of intelligence or skills
  - Etc.

Slide 11–7

Examples of Barriers (continued)

- Cultural
  - Taboos
  - Traditions
  - Excessive belief in logic and reason, numbers
  - Distrust of gut feelings
  - Etc.
- Expressive
  - Inadequate "language" skill in the subject
  - Using the wrong media
  - Communication skills related to others in the organization
  - Etc.

Slide 11–8

Application Exercise

- Use the handout and one of the decisions you listed in unit one. Classify which of the six categories of barriers you encountered (or may encounter) as you try to come to a decision.
- Discuss your answers with a neighbor or team mate.

Slide 11–9

Traits That Influence Decisions

- Which of the barriers listed earlier today relate to an individual?
- Which relate to an organization's culture or the work environment?

The next module will deal with how to overcome the barriers, once they have been identified.

Slide 11–10

Module 3 Summary

- Identify six kinds of barriers to effective decision making.
- Identify personal traits related to decision making.
- Identify group traits related to decision making.

Slide 11–11

Thank You for Your Attention

- Next meeting:
- Assignment:
- Other announcements?

Slide 11–12

Module 4—Overcoming Barriers to Creativity

Module 4 looks closely at ways to overcome the barriers to creativity that were identified in module 3. It is recommended for any session in which the training program lasts more than one day, and it needs to follow module 3 in sequence.

Training Objectives

After completing this module, the participants should be able to

♦   explain four techniques for overcoming barriers to decision making

♦   develop a personal plan for reducing at least two of the common barriers to creativity.

Module 4 Time

♦   Approximately 1 hour

Introduction, welcome, and review of previous modules	5 minutes
PowerPoint presentation and group discussion	30 minutes
Worksheet: application exercise	20 minutes
Wrap-up, learning check, and preview	5 minutes

Note: This includes time for a quick review at the start and a learning check at the end.

Materials

♦   Attendance list

♦   Pencils, pens, and paper for each participant

- Whiteboard or flipchart and markers

- Name tags or name tents for each participant

- Worksheet 12–1: Overcoming Creativity Barriers

- Computer, screen, and projector for displaying PowerPoint slides; alternatively, overhead projector and overhead transparencies

- PowerPoint slide program (slides 12–1 through 12–12)

- This chapter for reference or detailed facilitator notes

- Optional: music, coffee, or other refreshments.

Module Preparation

Arrive ahead of time to greet the participants, and make sure materials are available and laid out appropriately for the way you want to run the class.

Sample Agenda

0:00   Welcome the class.

Have slide 12–1 up on the screen as participants arrive; go to slide 12–2 as you begin.

Preview the agenda for this session (the objectives).

Ask for questions or concerns.

0:05   PPT Presentation.

Begin with slide 12–3; pause for discussion, then proceed through slide 12–9. (Note that slides 12–6 and 12–7 also include questions for discussion.)

0:35   Worksheets.

Distribute Worksheet 12–1: Overcoming Creativity Barriers.

Show slide 12–10 as the participants work on the worksheet.

Move among participants to keep them on task.

Have participants discuss answers with others.

0:55   Wrap-up.

Show slide 12–11. Review the objectives with participants.

Ask for questions.

Check for learning; questions can be in oral or printed form (see below).

Show slide 12–12. Dismiss the class.

Trainer's Notes

8:00 a.m. Welcome (5 minutes).

Show slide 12–1 as participants arrive.

Take care of housekeeping items.

8:05 a.m. Techniques for Overcoming Barriers to Creativity (30 minutes).

Show slide 12–2, and preview the topics in module 4.

Show slide 12–3.

Tell the participants that some of the reasons we don't exercise our creativity is that the organizational climate or personal barriers often discourage creativity. We may be afraid of making mistakes, or even of losing our jobs, if we are too creative.

How much an individual can personally do to change the climate depends in part on where he or she is within the organization's hierarchy. It also depends on that person's leadership skills. Someone who runs the organization (or a portion of it), probably can have a big influence on the climate. A person who is part of an employee group such as a self-managed work team (or participative management teams by whatever name) in an organization is probably open to the idea of change. But for most of us, changing the organizational climate is a difficult proposition.

Show slide 12–4. Review the Galbraith and Kettering quotes with the participants.

Show slide 12–5. Discuss with participants what that term means to them. It is explained on the following slide.

Show slide 12–6. Talk about organizational climate. The seminal work on organizational culture and climate was done by Edgar Schein. It's a whole college course in itself, so we're just going to define it enough to discuss how it affects decision making. (More about the organizational climate is covered in module 9.)

You can think of the organizational climate as the manner in which an organization operates. Look at the words used on this slide: beliefs, values, style, adapting to change, employee behavior, and so forth. These are all evidence of the organizational climate. Ask your learners: How do these things affect decision making in the organization?

Show slide 12–7.

Now talk about changing people's individual attitudes. People vary in their personal thirst for creativity. James L. Adams's list from module 3 helps make those reasons more obvious. The desire to be creative comes, at least in part, from an individual's early experiences in trying to be creative. If these experiences were successful and accepted, a person probably has more willingness to continue to try later in life to be more creative. If not, a person may be more comfortable conforming to the structured environment.

Resistance to creativity is normally an *attitude,* not a value. And attitudes can be changed with appropriate motivation.

Still, it is not enough to simply put someone into a situation that requires creativity and expect them to be creative. That's akin to just throwing someone into the water to teach them to swim. Blocks to creativity develop over a long period of time. Getting rid of the barriers requires that an individual do two things:

1. Identify the barriers that interfere with creativity. Bringing barriers to the conscious level allows people to analyze the barriers that operate for them. Adams's categories provide a good framework for the identification and analysis.

2. Decide to allow him- or herself the freedom to be creative and to get into situations that demand creativity. Practice in being creative can help. For example, one possible way to identify and analyze your own creativity barriers is to try some brain teasers, puzzles, or word games.

Once you've succeeded in one of the puzzles, ask yourself what got in the way of solving it sooner. Also, you might find it interesting and helpful to keep a record of things that kept you from being creative.

It's not enough to overcome the barriers you encountered with one particular problem. You must also understand the process you used to succeed quickly in others and how that process can be applied to the next situation. Otherwise, you've learned only for the one event.

Show slide 12–8.

Our purpose for encouraging creativity is pragmatic: We want to come up with a good list of viable options from which to evaluate and solve problems or make decisions that create effective management plans and controls.

Here is a list of techniques that can help make you a more creative person. We'll describe them one by one.

Practice. Try little things to build your creativity. Look at old things in new ways. Put yourself into situations where there's no clear response. Join a new group, try a new restaurant, take a new route to work. Visit an art gallery or a science museum. Try a new puzzle or game. Debate an issue. Building creativity doesn't require a major change in lifestyle; it requires a commitment to try to become more versatile in how you approach things.

Competition. For some people, competition is the extra motivation that spurs them to open up their own resources more effectively. It could be in the traditional sports sense of playing baseball or diving or skiing, or playing chess or poker. It could also be in artistic ways such as writing or photography contests. It could be competition in the business-career sense of working to make sure you're the one who gets the desired promotion. It could be competition in selling your company's products. It could be in the area of personal relationships—to win the girl or guy of your dreams or to settle the argument that "Mom always liked you best."

Mental Preparation. When we make our annual New Year's resolution to shape up physically, we are faced with the warnings from the medical profession: Get a check up, have a plan for your exercise program, get plenty of rest, eat healthy food, and be sure to "warm up" before undertaking strenuous exercise. That same kind of advice applies to developing mental capacities. For example, when you're over-tired or hungry, it's hard to think at all, let alone be more creative. Pacing yourself, getting enough rest, and eating properly, will help your creativity.

In a previous module, it was suggested that you try some brain-teasers or puzzles and keep track of the barriers you found that hinder you from solving them quickly. Part of mental preparation is knowing what barriers you've encountered before, so you can avoid them in the future.

Teams or Groups. Working as part of a group can sometimes help overcome barriers to creativity. Being around different personalities and viewpoints helps you look at things differently. (We'll cover more about solving problems in groups in module 9.)

Our brains are marvelous, and humans are among the very few species that actively pursue creativity. But some of the biggest gains in civilization came from humans learning to use tools to extend their own physical and mental capabilities. That's where this training is heading. First, why is creativity important, and then what are some tools we can use to enhance our creativity?

Show slide 12–9.

Most people today don't attempt to build a house without tools. A mud hut or lean-to shelter would be the best you might be accomplish without a collection of sophisticated tools. A saw, hammer, nails, and other tools make it much easier to build a far superior house.

A wide variety of creativity tools have been developed that can help us overcome Adams's barriers. These include many methods that are widely understood and used, such as brainstorming. Some of the most useful tools are so commonplace that most people don't even consider them to be creativity aids. Using checklists and catalogs, for example, are excellent ways to come up with options that might never have been developed or considered without them.

It may seem strange to hear me recommending tools that help *structure* a free-flowing process like creativity. That sounds paradoxical, yet it's true. Creativity tools are the subject of the next module.

8:35 a.m. Application Exercise (20 minutes).

Show slide 12–10, and review the anonymous quote. The point here is that once barriers to the decision process have been identified, as we hope happened in this module, the participants should be equipped with a variety of ways to deal with those barriers. That is the subject of the next module.

Show slide 12–11. Distribute Worksheet 12–1: Overcoming Creativity Barriers. Move among the participants to keep them on task.

INSTRUCTIONS FOR WORKSHEET 12–1: OVERCOMING CREATIVITY BARRIERS

Objective of the worksheet: This is the fourth in a series of worksheets that is presented in each training module. It incorporates one or two of the topics that were identified in the pretest by participants as examples of decisions they would soon need to make. Each participant will work throughout all the sessions (up to 10, depending on the length of the program) on his or her personally chosen topics. If one topic has been chosen by a group, rather than an individual, the sheet can be completed by one person for the group based on its discussion of the questions.

Time required: Approximately 20 minutes.

Instructor guidance: The questions on the worksheet refer to overcoming creativity barriers as covered in module 4.

Ask the participants to consider how organizational climate influences the decision(s) on which they are working. For example, the decision may require a new way of doing something that has "always been done some other way." What climate barriers are there, and what can be done to address them? Then move on to the individual attitude barriers. If an individual participant or someone else involved in the decision is having difficulty coming up with ideas, suggest an exercise that might loosen their way of thinking. For example, would it help if the individual visited another company to see how they deal with the issue, or if the person read a book or article about ways to deal with the decision?

Next, have the participants consider if there are any skills or tools of which they're aware that would help them overcome any creativity barriers. This may be more challenging because tools have not yet been discussed. (They are covered in the next module.)

The key point to this exercise is to get the participants to clearly identify some barriers that they may need to overcome as they work toward decisions on the issues they have identified.

Walk among the participants during the 20 minutes allowed and try to keep them on task. If some participants finish early, encourage them to work with someone else who has a different decision to work on. If some are not finished by the end of the time, have them continue to think about it and complete the worksheet before the next meeting. The next session will build on the answers the participants have recorded on this worksheet and will suggest some tools that can be used.

Wrap-up: At the end of the allotted time, have the participants keep the worksheets. If the next module is presented on a different day, instruct them to bring the worksheets back with them.

8:55 a.m. Module 4 Summary (5 minutes).

Show slide 12–12. Note that the second objective is covered by Worksheet 12–1.

LEARNING CHECK QUESTIONS

You can use the learning check questions and answers in oral or printed form.

Discussion Questions

◆ Name some things individuals can do to increase their creativity.

Answer: Change organizational climate, change individual attitudes, develop personal creativity skills, learn and use appropriate creativity "tools."

◆ If you were to walk into an organization, what are some visual clues that might help you find out about its culture?

Answer: orderliness and cleanliness, business layout, adaptation to change, employee dress and behavior, public documents, formality, and so forth.

◆ What are some things you can do to help increase your creativity?

Answer: Looking at old things in new ways. For example, taking a new route to work, joining a new group, trying a new restaurant, or going to an old restaurant but sitting somewhere different and ordering a different meal. Visiting an art gallery or a science museum. Taking a class in creativity. Working on puzzles or games also can stimulate some creativity, as can debating issues with other people.

True or False Questions

◆ We can enhance our creativity by using structured tools.

Answer: True

◆ Resistance to creativity is normally part of an individual's value system.

Answer: False. It's an attitude.

Creativity Stimulators

Optional exercise: Add 5–10 minutes.

If you have any extra time, you may distribute Worksheet 12–2: Creativity Stimulators. Give the participants time to complete the puzzles, and then discuss how participants came up with the answers.

9:00 a.m. Thank You for Your Attention.

Show slide 12–13. Edit this slide to include information relevant to your class.

Worksheet 12–1
Overcoming Creativity Barriers

Restate the decision you're working on _____

Take out the worksheet from module 3 where you identified possible barriers that could affect your decision. What can be done to overcome these barriers?

Change the organizational climate. Are there supportive people high enough within the organization's hierarchy? Is there good leadership? Is the organization open to the idea of change? How entrenched is the culture?

Change your individual attitude. Get away from "we've always done it that way" and other negative mindsets. Be willing to get the input of others. Be less defensive.

continued on next page

Worksheet 12–1, continued

Overcoming Creativity Barriers

Increase your personal creativity. Try some brain teasers or puzzles and keep track of the barriers. Mental preparation includes practice and knowing what barriers you've encountered before so you can avoid them. Look at old things in new ways, and put yourself into situations where there's no clear response.

Learn to use some creativity tools: brainstorming, catalogs and checklists, attribute listing, forced connections, doodling, and so forth.

Notes:

Worksheet 12–2
Creativity Stimulators

Use the following exercises to stimulate creativity in your learners.

Using the nine dots in the square below, draw four straight lines connected at the end, which go through all nine dots. (Don't lift your pencil.)

○   ○   ○

○   ○   ○

○   ○   ○

In the following line of letters, cross out six letters so that the remaining letters, without altering their sequence, will spell a familiar English word.

B S A I N X L E A T N T E A R S

Complete the following equations by choosing the appropriate words represented by the letters. For example, 16 = O. in a P. would be "ounces - pound."

26 = L. of the A. _____

1001 = A. N. _____

3 = B.M. (S.H.T.R.) _____

1 = W. on a U. _____

7 = W. of the A. W. _____

11 = P. on a F. T. _____

12 = S. of the Z. _____

18 = H. on a G. C. _____

13 = S. on the A. F. _____

continued on next page

Worksheet 12–2, continued
Creativity Stimulators

Answers

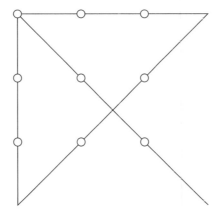

One of several possibilities. People think they can't go beyond the imaginary box around the lines.

Cross out S̶I̶X̶L̶E̶T̶T̶E̶R̶S̶ and the remaining ones spell BANANA.

26 letters of the alphabet

1001 Arabian nights

3 blind mice (see how they run)

1 wheel on a unicycle

7 wonders of the ancient world

11 players on a football team

12 signs of the zodiac

18 holes on a golf course

13 stripes on the American flag

MAKING EFFECTIVE DECISIONS

Module 4
Overcoming Barriers to Creativity

Slide 12–1

Module 4 Topics

- Explain four techniques for overcoming barriers to decision making.
- Develop a personal plan for reducing at least two common barriers.

Slide 12–2

Techniques for Overcoming Barriers to Creativity

- Change the organizational climate.
- Change individual attitudes
- Develop personal creativity skills.
- Learn and use appropriate creativity "tools."

Slide 12–3

Thoughts About Creativity Blocks

- "Faced with a choice between changing one's mind and proving that there's no need to do so, almost everybody gets busy on the proof."
  — John Kenneth Galbraith

- "If you have always done it that way, it is probably wrong."
  — Charles Kettering

Slide 12–4

Change the Organizational Climate

Slide 12–5

Organizational Climate

- Organizations have their own "personalities" that come out of their
  - Beliefs, values, style, and assumptions
- Evidences of the organizational climate
  - Working environment, business layout, adaptation to change, employee dress and behavior, public documents, formality, etc.
- How does this affect decision making?

Slide 12–6

Change Individual Attitudes

- Just like organizations, individuals vary in their beliefs, values, assumptions, and way of operating.
- Which of the barriers to creativity from the last unit are big influences in your own decision-making style?
- How can you reduce those barriers?

Slide 12–7

Develop Personal Skills

Some techniques that may help include...

- Practice in identifying and overcoming barriers that affect you
- Competition
- Mental preparation
- Using teams or groups

Slide 12–8

Learn and Use Tools

Slide 12–9

Thoughts About Decision Making

- "If your only tool is a hammer, you tend to see all problems as nails. Having a versatile, well-stocked toolbox is essential for good decision making."

—Anonymous

Slide 12–10

Application Exercise

- Complete Worksheet 12–1 and discuss it with others in the group.

Slide 12–11

Module 4 Review

- Explain four techniques for overcoming barriers to decision making.
- Develop a personal plan for reducing at least two common barriers.

Slide 12–12

Thank You for Your Attention

- Next meeting:
- Assignment:
- Other announcements?

Slide 12–13

◆

Module 5—Tools to Improve Creativity

Module 5 describes a number of tools that can help improve creativity.

Training Objectives

After completing this module, the participants should be able to

*   describe and use at least five tools that may help improve creativity

*   apply the appropriate tools to a variety of situations that require creativity.

Module 5 Time

*   Approximately 2 hours

Note: This schedule includes time for a quick review at the start and a learning check at the end. It also includes a constant back and forth of presentations and exercises. As with all sessions of more than 90 minutes, a 10-minute break is included.

Materials

*   Attendance list

*   Pencils, pens, and paper for each participant

*   Whiteboard or flipchart and markers

*   Name tags or name tents for each participant

*   Worksheet 13–1: Brainstorming Techniques

*   Worksheet 13–2: Checklists and Catalogs

*   Worksheet 13–3: Attribute Listing

◆ Worksheet 13–4: Cause-Effect Fishbone Diagrams

◆ Worksheet 13–5: Cause-Effect Matrix Diagrams

◆ Worksheet 13–6: Morphological Analysis

◆ Worksheet 13–7: Decision-Making Worksheet for Module 5

◆ Computer, screen, and projector for displaying PowerPoint slides; alternatively, overhead projector and overhead transparencies

◆ PowerPoint slide program (slides 13–1 through 13–24)

◆ This chapter for reference or detailed facilitator notes

◆ Optional: music, coffee or other refreshments.

Module Preparation

Arrive ahead of time to greet the participants and make sure materials are available and laid out for the way you want to run the class.

Sample Agenda

Note: Because of the nature of the material in this module, the sample agenda has much more detailed schedule suggestions. Unlike previous modules where the presentation is followed by an extended time for one worksheet exercise, we suggest here that the seven exercises be integrated into the presentation so they are completed immediately after the discussion of that particular process. A lot of material is included, so you will need to keep the participants on track fairly closely. All times are still just recommendations, and if you as the trainer believe that your participants are not able to assimilate this as scheduled, then either plan to extend the suggested two-hour timeframe or delete one or two of the creativity tools along with their associated exercises.

0:00   Welcome class.

Have slide 13–1 on the screen as the participants arrive; go to slide 13–2 as you begin the session.

Preview the agenda for this session (the objectives).

Ask for questions or concerns.

0:05   PPT presentation with exercises.

Begin with slide 13–3 and proceed through slide 13–9 with a combination of presentation followed by application exercises for the "creativity tools" being discussed.

0:20   Worksheet 13–1.

Show slide 13–10; distribute Worksheet 13–1: Creativity Tools.

Have class apply the presentation on brainstorming using worksheet.

0:30   PPT presentation and Worksheet 13–2.

Show slide 13–11 and discuss; show slide 13–12.

Distribute Worksheet 13–2: Checklists and Catalogs, and conduct exercise.

0:40   PPT presentation and Worksheet 13–3.

Show slide 13–13 and discuss; show slide 13–14.

Distribute Worksheet 13–3: Attribute Listing, and conduct exercise.

0:50   Break.

Pause at a convenient stopping point for a 7- to 10-minute break.

1:00   PPT presentation and Worksheet 13–4

Show slides 13–15 and 13–16 and discuss; show slide 13–17.

Distribute Worksheet 13–4: Cause-Effect Wishbone Diagrams, and conduct exercise.

1:15   PPT presentation and Worksheet 13–5.

Show slide 13–18 and discuss; show slide 13–19.

Distribute Worksheet 13–5: Cause-Effect Matrix Diagrams, and conduct exercise.

1:25   PPT presentation and Worksheet 13–6.

Show slide 13–20 and discuss; show slide 13–21.

Distribute Worksheet 13–6: Morphological Analysis, and conduct exercise.

1:40   PPT presentation and worksheet.

Show slide 13–22: Application Exercise. Distribute Worksheet 13–7 and have participants work on exercise.

1:55   Wrap-up.

Show slide 13–23. Review the objectives with participants.

Ask for questions.

Check for learning (questions can be in oral or printed form—see below).

2:00   Show slide 13–24. Edit this slide to show appropriate information. Dismiss the class.

Trainer's Notes

8:00 a.m. Welcome (5 minutes).

Show slide 13–1.

Welcome participants and take care of housekeeping items.

Show slide 13–2, and preview the two module 5 objectives.

8:05 a.m. Creativity Tools (25 minutes).

Show slide 13–3. State the following to the participants: This module will be a little different from the previous four, in that we're going to talk about and then practice each of these creativity-enhancing tools one at a time. Probably many of you have been involved in brainstorming sessions, although they are often done in ways that don't tap the full potential of this technique. We'll talk about how to do it in the most effective way, then give you a brief chance to practice it. After that, we'll spend a few minutes on how using catalogs and checklists can improve your creativity. Then we'll introduce three techniques that many of you may find unfamiliar: (1) attribute listing, (2) cause-effect analysis (two types), and (3) morphological analysis. These are all creativity-enhancing techniques that can cause us to look at problems and decisions in a different way. First, let's consider the process of brainstorming.

Show slide 13–4. Talk about the following requirements for successful brainstorming:

◆ ***Small-size group (four to nine people preferred).*** Groups smaller than four or larger than 10 people become awkward and less productive. Larger groups should be subdivided. Smaller groups might try some other techniques or temporarily add other people who might have some worthwhile perspective on the problem.

◆ ***Mixed group (not homogeneous).*** Homogeneous groups tend to produce fewer creative ideas. When possible, for brainstorming use a group that varies in background, gender, age, job category, and so forth. The diversity will usually enhance the creativity generated.

◆ ***No evaluation of ideas (at this point we want quantity, not quality).*** Quantity of ideas is the goal. This means that you go for volume, not quality of ideas. In going for quantity we may collect some good ideas that otherwise would be missed. We'll judge the quality of the ideas as the next step in the decision-making process, not now. Evaluating the ideas at this point tends to inhibit people from being free-flowing with their suggestions.

◆ ***Limited time frame.*** A brainstorming session should last 15 minutes at least and 45 minutes at most.

◆ ***Don't discuss the issue ahead of time.*** It may stifle new ideas during the brainstorming session.

◆ ***Tolerance for "out-of-the-box" thinking.*** Sometimes throwing out a few completely off-the-wall ideas will loosen up a group and encourage alternative viewpoints. Some leaders start with a "silliness" session to get the creativity juices flowing. (It doesn't work for everyone, though.)

Show slide 13–5. Talk about the job of the brainstorming leader.

Tips for the brainstorming leader:

◆ Make sure all participants know and follow the ground rules.

◆ Use warm-up techniques to get the group participating. This just means getting the group to talk with each other, perhaps by doing a practice brainstorm on a really simple topic such as a gift for the boss or where to go on their next vacation.

◆ Define the problem and set the structure by which you'll proceed. You'll need to specifically state what problem the group is to work on, such as: "We're looking for new ways to increase customer traffic in our Highland store." Make sure everyone is focused on the correct issue before starting.

◆ Keep the discussion "on track." If someone in the group begins to criticize another's idea or goes off on a tangent that's not related to the issue at hand, step in and restate the issue that's being brainstormed. The analysis and fine-tuning come later, not during the initial session.

◆ Record ideas in a way they can be viewed by the group (flipchart, whiteboard, computer display).

◆ If you paraphrase as you write an idea, confirm with the person who offered the idea that you've captured the essence of what they intended.

◆ Participate yourself, add ideas of your own if desired, but don't judge or edit the ideas offered by the class.

Show slide 13–6. Note that the dynamics of brainstorming sessions can inhibit some participants. Skillful leadership is needed to ensure that everyone contributes to creating an effective list of alternatives. Keep in mind the factors that can inhibit the effectiveness of group interactions:

◆ Presence of an expert or a high-level manager can discourage some people from voicing their ideas.

◆ Too much play or getting off track can discourage some participants.

◆ Criticism or negative thinking, even subtle, can ruin the effectiveness of the process.

◆ Homogeneity of the group, where all think alike or have worked together before, can inhibit creativity.

Effective leadership and skilled facilitation are essential. Note that brainstorming doesn't work well for decisions with high risk or uncertainty.

Show slide 13–7. Discuss the following variations on traditional brainstorming:

Structured brainstorming. Once the problem has been described, each person is asked to contribute one idea at a time in turn. If participants don't have an idea, they pass. This continues until everyone has passed in the same round.

Problems such as one person dominating the discussion and others not contributing can be addressed with structured brainstorming.

Nominal group technique. This technique can allow individual creativity to work before it becomes inhibited by the group. This process requires people to think silently, at first, writing down their ideas. They then contribute to the list in round-robin style. As ideas are voiced, anyone can question the contribution to clarify what is meant, but should not challenge or analyze it. The nominal group technique can end with a voting process, which asks people to choose their favorite ideas (one to five), thereby giving the group a sense of which ideas are popular. This voting narrows down the number of options to consider in the next decision-making step and actually begins the analysis phase.

Gordon Technique. When the subject or problem seems to have one or a few "obvious" solutions, the Gordon Technique can crack through the conventional thinking that is inhibiting creativity. For example, if we face a problem that's always been dealt with in one way, it's natural to block out other ways of handling it.

Using the Gordon Technique, the group is asked for ideas about a subject that is *known in detail only to the leader*. The leader begins with a very broad and abstract definition of the problem and starts to take ideas. Then, the leader narrows the statement through several stages, each time retaining previous suggestions, which still apply to the narrower statement.

Brainwriting. Each participant writes down his or her ideas about the problem under discussion. Participants then pass what they've written to someone else in the group. That person elaborates on what was written and adds any ideas of his or her own. Throughout brainwriting, participants are encouraged to combine ideas, improve on each others' ideas, and hitchhike on things already suggested.

Repeat until everyone in the group has had a chance to contribute to everyone else's original ideas.

Show slide 13–8. Now talk about how to use the ideas from the brainstorming session.

The purpose of brainstorming is to create an extensive list of ideas, and because evaluation during brainstorming is prohibited, the result is lots of ideas, including many that are impractical or impossible to use.

Eliminate truly unworkable ideas. To make the list of ideas usable, the ideas must be objectively evaluated. The first step in evaluation is to eliminate any truly unworkable ideas. A word of caution: Any person who makes the decision to eliminate an idea will approach it with his or her biases. With that in mind, it's important to be sure an idea is actually unworkable before it's eliminated. For example, just because some members of the group have never tweeted and are unfamiliar with Twitter, doesn't mean using Twitter as a means to increase business should not be considered. Different generations have different needs and may not understand all the suggestions that come up. The same is true for people with other demographic diversity.

Group similar deas. The purpose of grouping is to determine what information needs to be collected to evaluate the ideas, and where the same information can be used on more than one evaluation.

Set priority for data-gathering and further evaluations. A priority should be established as to which ideas get evaluated first. The basis for the priority might be cost (which ideas are cheapest to implement), likelihood of success, or ease of evaluation, for example.

Key questions at this point: (1) What to do with the narrowed-down list of ideas? and (2) Who does the evaluation of those "finalist" ideas?

Group evaluation of the ideas—If the analysis needed to choose the best idea isn't too complicated and the cost isn't too high, it may be practical to extend the brainstorming to narrow down the options or even choose which idea to use. One way is just to take a vote of the brainstorming group.

Let's say that 45 ideas were generated by brainstorming. The leader could ask everyone to choose the five ideas they think will work best. After everyone has had time to choose their five favorites, a vote is taken on each item with each person getting five votes. The result is a list of favorites, based on which ideas got the most votes.

Note: Voting on the ideas will work well only when the group has adequate information to make an evaluation. It is a popularity contest among the ideas, rather than a quantitative or objective evaluation. But if some of the most popular ideas will actually work to solve the problem, and the cost is not too high, then the most popular idea might be a reasonable choice.

Show slide 13–9. This slide is a "quickie." It deserves only a brief comment, something like: "It's good to keep in mind that at this point, before evaluation, that there may be more than one 'right' answer."

Show slide 13–10. Distribute Worksheet 13–1: Brainstorming Techniques.

Use Worksheet 13–1 or pick a volunteer to apply brainstorming to a decision he or she faces.

The worksheet includes definitions of the four types of brainstorming only so the participants have this information in writing to take with them. The simplest to use is structured brainstorming, and time is limited. You might want to act as leader, or choose one of the participants whom you believe can do a good job. Follow the directions you've just covered, such as group size (make two groups if you have too many in the class), and so forth. Do not go beyond just demonstrating how many ideas can be generated; that is, don't try to narrow the list down to the best final decision. Move on to the next topic by 30 minutes into the training session.

8:30 a.m. Checklists and Catalogs (10 minutes).

Show slide 13–11.

Overview—checklists. First, we want to talk about the types of checklists that are useful in decision making.

Typical checklists might deal with: items you'll need for vacation; how to set up your computer; what automobile maintenance services are needed at 36,000 miles; what groceries you might need for the week; and so forth.

Checklists can be inductive or deductive; that is, they can help you either create options or evaluate them, depending on the nature of the checklist.

Inductive checklists require a step-by-step approach (such as putting together the swing set you bought your child), whereas *deductive* checklists serve as preconstructed brainstorming lists with the items listed in no specific sequence.

For decision making, any preconstructed list of points to consider is a checklist. A list of points to consider is valuable in two ways: (1) if you made the list, you can return to it make sure you don't skip points that need attention, and (2) if someone else made the checklist, you can take advantage their ideas on the subject,

Where do you find effective checklists for the subject you're interested in? Common sources include textbooks on the subject, published articles on the subject, advertisements about a product or service, owner's or instruction manuals, and so forth.

How do checklists help in decision making? Using checklists helps the decision maker add structure to both the creative or analytical processes. Checklists provide a means to use others' thinking to help the process along. Checklists also provide additional suggestions for consideration in specific applications.

Overview—catalogs. Using catalogs is another way to come up with additional options and alternatives to any decision-making or problem-solving issue. It allows the decision maker to tap into already created lists, some of which will probably expand in unexpected ways.

A "catalog" may come in a variety of forms: directories, the classified section of a magazine or newspaper, databases, and many others. If your problem or decision is of major importance, it will be worth your time to visit a library or contact an individual or organization that specializes in relevant research. But you might first consider sources such as these:

Professional or industry associations in the area you're researching. For example, if you need materials about training skills, contact organizations such as The American Society for Training & Development, National Education Association, and so on. Your library probably has a directory of associations, which can give you some leads.

Commercial research databases can provide names of companies and agencies that help with your decision. You can find them by searching on keywords.

Industrial directories include Moody's or Dun and Bradstreet, along with many others that a librarian can help you find. They contain lists of companies you can contact for product or service details that may help with your decision.

The most obvious sources for most people these days are Google, Yahoo!, Ask.com, and the myriad other search engines available online.

Show slide 13–12. Distribute copies of Worksheet 13–2: Checklists and Catalogs.

This worksheet includes definitions only so that the participants will have them available when they leave the session. The important part for this exercise is to have each participant or each group answer the question at the bottom: "For the decision you're working on, where might you find useful checklists or catalogs?" This question can probably be answered in less than two minutes. Then move quickly on to the next topic.

8:40 a.m. Attribute Listing (10 minutes).

Show slide 13–13. If you follow the script below, you'll need a ballpoint pen. You'll also need to practice disassembling it before the class, so the demonstration goes well. But you don't *have* to use a ballpoint pen. You can substitute some other object you can disassemble to make the same points.

Overview—attribute listing. Attribute listing is a means to evaluate and improve physical items. Although it can also be used with abstract concepts, it's more difficult. Attribute listing is based on the premise that we think about parts differently than we think about wholes. This tool can be used by either an individual or a group. If done by a group, it can be used in combination with brainstorming concepts.

The phrase, "You can't see the forest for the trees," fits here. This technique is designed to force you to look at both the trees and the forest. It can help you overcome perception problems, which block creativity.

The "divide-to-conquer" process has its roots in Frederick Taylor's application of the scientific method to the study of production. Taylor didn't try to improve the process of coal shoveling—he improved several of its individual components; and, as a result of his improvements, the whole process was improved.

For attribute listing, it always helps to have the physical item available for reference.

Choose an object that you can easily disassemble. A click-top ballpoint pen works well. Take it apart into its pieces and ask what you can do with each component. The barrel could be used as a straw or a small blowgun or a whistle (when you blow across it like a bottle top). The ink chamber can be used with the barrel and internal spring to be a small "rocket launcher." The clip can be used as a tie clip, or noisemaker when you push the button up and down. What other ideas can the participants come up with?

Show slide 13–14, and distribute Worksheet 13–3: Attribute Listing.

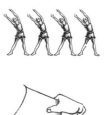

This worksheet has the definition of attribute listing so that the participants will have it available when they leave the session. It will be simpler to use a physical object of some sort to do this exercise. If you have an advanced group of participants, you might choose the second option on the sheet of trying to break apart a decision.

8:50 a.m. Break (10 minutes).

Encourage them to return promptly, because there are still four more brief exercises to complete in this module.

9:00 a.m. Cause-Effect Analysis (25 minutes).

Show slide 13–15.

Overview—cause-effect analysis. We use cause-effect analysis to find and confirm relationships between facts. The "cause" part can be used to help search for causes of problems (variances from standard results). The "effect" part can be used to help project what might happen as a result of implementing a particular plan. These diagrams can also be used to help organize brainstorming as it is being done.

Cause-effect analyses can be done in a variety of ways. Some of the techniques result in a cause-effect diagram that can be used to help organize brainstorming as it is being done, but much of the value of cause-effect analysis to get down on paper the "facts" and to show among them relationships as we believe them to exist. Having the facts related visually as causes and effects helps us follow the logic and test relationships for reasonableness.

Cause-effect diagrams use a graphical format of lines and tables that represent a relationship between an effect and its causes or a cause and its resulting effects. They can be used to: (1) recognize important causes, (2) understand all effects and causes, (3) compare operational procedures, (4) improve processes, and (5) determine options or possible solutions.

These tools are frequently taught as part of a total quality management programs. We will cover two types of cause-effect analysis: fishbone diagrams and matrices (also called Johari windows).

Show slide 13–16.

Fishbone Diagrams: One of the most common formats for cause-effect analyses looks something like a fish skeleton, hence the name "fishbone."

Explain that the fishbone diagram on slide 13–16 is of a production problem: The ball bearings being produced are too small.

The major possible causes (material, the method being used, the workers, and the machinery) are listed in boxes placed parallel to and some distance from the main arrow. Arrows slanting toward the main arrow or production line connect the boxes.

The minor possible causes are connected to the major causes on lines or arrows pointing into the major causes.

Show slide 13–17. Distribute Worksheet 13–4: Cause-Effect Fishbone Diagrams.

Direct participants to use the worksheet to analyze a decision that they or a colleague is working on.

After allowing participants time to fill in the worksheet, review the results and ask for their thoughts about using a fishbone diagram to help solve a problem or make a decision.

Show slide 13–18.

Cause-effect matrix. This is typically a two-by-two grid that shows relationships between items.

Use the following example: We are investigating whether there is a cause-effect relationship between being female and liking horses. We define "being female" as the possible cause, and "liking horses" as the effect. Then we talk with 40 people and ask if they're female (be prepared for nasty comments if you have to ask), and if they like horses. We then tally the results in each box according to the answers. If we have taken an honest sample, we can imply a rather strong cause-effect relationship from this data.

Show slide 13–19. Distribute copies of Worksheet 13–5: Cause-Effect Matrix Diagrams.

If the participants can come up with a suitable topic for this analysis, it's best to do it on a flipchart or whiteboard (rather than on the worksheet). You could ask the participants, for example, if they use Twitter or text on their cell phones and divide them into under- and over-30 years of age. See if being under 30 has a cause-effect relationship to the use of Twitter. Use your imagination to come up with examples that will work with this creativity tool for your particular group of participants.

9:25 a.m. Morphological Analysis (15 minutes).

Show slide 13–20. Another useful decision-making tool is morphological analysis.

Literally, the name means "analysis of structure." This tool gives you a process to analyze the structure of a decision. You break the decision into its major component parts. Once the structure is analyzed, forced-relationship techniques are used in order to produce extensive combinations of ideas. It forces you to put things together in ways you might never have considered without using this process.

How many parts should the problem be divided into? A table of four variables with ten choices each would result in 10,000 combinations. It quickly becomes apparent why limiting the choices and variables is necessary, because you must decide on the merits of each combination individually. Think, for example, of a computer program designed to come up with passwords. If you have 26 letters and 10 digits (ignoring symbols for the moment), a six-character password with options from "AAAAAA" to "000000" would have 1,947,792 possible combinations. We will discuss how to calculate this in module 7.

You must know the component parts of a decision to be made or problem to be solved. You might use attribute listing or cause-effect analysis to determine components, although they may be somewhat obvious.

Show slide 13–21. Distribute copies of Worksheet 13–6: Morphological Analysis.

After allowing participants time to answer the questions on the worksheet, review the results and ask for their thoughts about using morphological analysis to help them make a decision.

9:40 a.m. Creativity Tools (15 minutes).

Show slide 13–22. Distribute Worksheet 13–7: Decision-Making Worksheet for Module 5.

Have the participants complete the worksheet individually or in groups. Move among them to keep them on task.

9:55 Module 5 Summary (5 minutes).

Show slide 13–23. Review the objectives covered in this module.

LEARNING CHECK QUESTIONS

You can use the learning check questions and answers in oral or printed form.

Discussion Questions

- ◆ Describe advantages and disadvantages of traditional brainstorming.

    Answer: Advantages: It's easy to do, it's creative, and ideas build off one another. Members feel involved, it encourages participant commitment to chiose, and so on. Disadvances: See slide 13–6.

- ◆ Name two different approaches to cause-effect analysis.

    Answer: fishbone diagrams and cause-effect matrix (or Johari windows diagram).

- ◆ What are potential problems with both the checklist and catalog techniques?

    Answers: (1) Difficulty in finding useful checklists and catalogs. (2) Collecting too much information.

- ◆ Between attribute listing and morphological analysis, which one forces combinations and which one forces separations?

Answer: Morphological analysis forces combinations, even though it requires breaking things apart first. Attribute listing requires you to break things apart.

◆ In the movie (or book) *Apollo 13*, the crew in space needed to create air filters to fit one unit, using materials from another and from things they had in the space capsule. On the ground, a group of engineers was brought into a room and told, "We have to make one of these (the functioning air filter) using only these materials (a stack of everything which was in the capsule that was expendable)." Would attribute listing or morphological analysis be best for this?

Answer: Both would be useful. Certain things could be broken apart so that only part of them would be used, but it's also necessary to put things together in new and different ways.

Multiple Choice Questions

1. "Fishbone diagrams" are one of several categories of

   a. Brainstorming

   b. Morphological analysis

   c. Cause-effect analysis *(answer)*

   d. Culinary techniques

2. A typical "Chinese menu," which requires choosing one item from column A and one item from column B, and so forth, is the basic idea behind which of the creativity tools?

   a. Cause-effect analysis

   b. Catalog technique

   c. Morphological analysis *(answer)*

   d. Brainstorming

   10:00 a.m. Thank You for Your Attention.

   Show slide 13–24. Edit the slide to include information relevant to your class. Dismiss the class.

Worksheet 13–1
Brainstorming Techniques

Four brainstorming techniques are discussed in the training:

Structured Brainstorming: Once the issue has been described, each person is asked to contribute one idea at a time in turn. If someone doesn't have an idea, he or she passes. Continue until everyone has had a turn in the same round.

Nominal Group Technique: The group is instructed to think silently, first writing down ideas. Participants then contribute to the list in round-robin style. Each person can question the contribution to clarify what is meant, but should not challenge or analyze it. The nominal group technique also ends with a voting process, which asks people to choose their favorite one to five ideas.

Gordon Technique (reverse brainstorming): The group is called together to come up with ideas about a subject known only to the leader. The leader starts with a very broad and abstract definition of the problem, and then narrows the statement through several stages, each time retaining previous suggestions that still apply.

Brainwriting is a variation in which each person gets a sheet of paper and anonymously writes his or her ideas on the question under discussion, then passes the sheet on to the next person, who elaborates and adds any more of his or her own ideas, suggested by what is already listed. The sheet continues around until all people have contributed to each original list.

Follow the guidelines discussed in class, and brainstorm about what to get your spouse or best friend for his or her birthday or another idea suggested by you or one of the other participants. Use the space below for notes.

Worksheet 13–2
Checklists and Catalogs

Checklists

Like several of the other tools in this unit, checklists can be either inductive or deductive. They can therefore be used either to create options or to evaluate them, depending on the nature of the checklist. Some checklists require a step-by-step approach, whereas others essentially serve as preconstructed brainstorming lists and require no specific sequence. Both types can be useful.

Typical checklists might deal with items you'll need for vacation; how to set up your computer; what automobile maintenance is needed at 36,000 miles; or what groceries you might need for the week. Essentially, any preconstructed list of points to consider is a checklist. They can be beneficial because they are reusable and allow you to take advantage of other people's ideas on the subject (or your own previous ideas).

Catalogs

The catalog technique helps a person come up with additional options and alternatives to almost any decision-making issue. It allows the decision maker to tap into already created lists, some of which will probably expand in unexpected ways.

Note that what is being called a "catalog" may come in a variety of guises: directories, the classified section of a magazine or newspaper, databases, and so forth, as well as the more traditional meaning of the word. The most obvious sources for most people these days would be to use the web search engines, such as *Google*, *Yahoo!*, *Ask.com*, and so forth.

For the decision you're working on, where might you find useful checklists or catalogs?

Worksheet 13–3
Attribute Listing

Attribute listing is a means to evaluate and improve physical items. Although this technique can be used with abstract concepts, it's more difficult. Attribute listing is based on the premise that we think about parts differently than we think about wholes. This tool can be used by either an individual or a group. If done by a group, it can be used in combination with brainstorming concepts.

The phrase, "You can't see the forest for the trees," fits here. This technique is designed to force you to look at both the trees and the forest. It can help you overcome perception problems that block creativity.

Try out the technique by taking a simple object such as a ball point pen or a wallet. If the decision you are trying to make has multiple parts to it, try breaking it into its components and then deal with each part separately. Option: Use a decision that one of your colleagues is working with and help him or her break it into pieces.

Worksheet 13–4
Cause-Effect Fishbone Diagrams

Cause-effect analyses can be done in a variety of ways. Their purpose is to find and confirm relationships between facts. The "cause" part can be used to help search for causes of problems (variances from standard) in control. The "effect" part can be used to help project what might happen as a result of implementing decisions. These diagrams can be used to help organize brainstorming as it is being done. Further, much of the value of these tools is to get down on paper the "facts" and relationships as we believe them to exist. The visual diagram helps to follow the logic and test it for reasonableness.

Use the "effect" fishbone diagram below to analyze the possible effects of the decision you have been working on (or some other decision suggested by your trainer or a colleague). The major branches are often designated as "people," "equipment," and so forth. Make up your own classifications to fit the issue at hand.

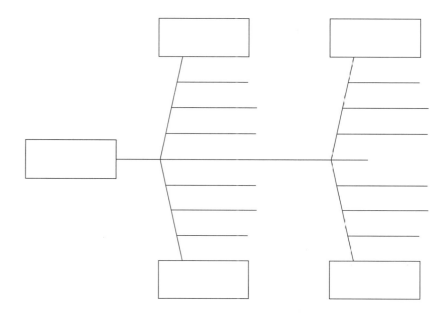

Worksheet 13–5
Cause-Effect Matrix Diagrams

Cause-effect analyses can be done in a variety of ways. Their purpose is to find and confirm relationships between facts. The "cause" part can be used to help search for causes of problems (variances from standard) in control. The "effect" part can be used to help project what might happen as a result of implementing decisions. These diagrams can be used to help organize brainstorming as it is being done. Further, much of the value of these tools is to get down on paper the "facts" and relationships as we believe them to exist. Having a visual diagram helps to follow the logic and test it for reasonableness.

Matrix (Johari window) Cause-effect matrices give a quick visual summary of the results of data analyses, and can suggest relationships, or lack thereof, between potential cause and effect.

Use the matrix diagram below to analyze the relationship between cause and effect. You'll have to collect data from the group or use your memory. For example: 1. Cause—Being rich; Effect—Being arrogant. List ten relatives or acquaintances you know and think of each one at a time. If they're both rich and arrogant, mark them in the cause occurs/effect occurs boxes. And so on.

Cause → Effect ↓	Cause Occurs	Cause Does Not Occur
Effect Occurs		
Effect Does Not Occur		

Worksheet 13–6
Morphological Analysis

Literally, the name means "analysis of structure." This tool gives you a process to analyze the structure of possible options for a decision. This means you break the decision into its major component parts. Once the structure is analyzed, forced relationship techniques are used to produce extensive combinations of ideas.

The example below offers options that could be considered for advertising special occasion meals a restaurant might make available. Which of the options make sense? You need to match each occasion with each possible combination of prospect and advertising medium. Some will make sense, but many won't. It simply forces you to think of combinations you might not have considered before. How many options are created by this technique? (*Hint:* Multiply the number of options in each column times each other, or O's times P's times AM's.)

Occasion	Prospect	Ad Medium
Mother's Day	Children	Radio advertisement
Valentine's Day	Lovers	Parking lot flyers
Birthday	Parents	Newspaper ad
Anniversary	Teachers	Airport display
	Executives	Cable TV spot
	Senior citizens	

How many options can be created from the table above? _____

How many options would be possible if there were 10 choices in each column? _____

Which of the above seems to make the most sense? _____

Worksheet 13–7
Decision-Making Worksheet for Module 5

Creativity Tools

Restate the decision(s) you have been working on during the training:

_____

Pick any two of the creativity tools discussed that would help to develop options for your decision:

- Brainstorming
- Catalogs and checklists
- Attribute listing
- Cause-effect analysis
- Morphological analysis

Then use the tools to come up with some possible options for yourself, and write them in the space below.

MAKING EFFECTIVE DECISIONS

Module 5

Tools to Improve Creativity

Slide 13–1

Module 5 Topics

- Describe and use at least five simple tools that may help improve creativity.
- Apply the appropriate tools to a variety of situations that require creativity.

Slide 13–2

Creativity Tools

- Brainstorming
- Checklists and catalogs
- Attribute listing
- Cause-effect analysis
- Morphological analysis

Slide 13–3

Requirements for Brainstorming

- Small size group (4–9 people preferred)
- Mixed group (not homogeneous)
- No evaluation of ideas (quantity, not quality)
- Limited time frame
- Limited previous discussion
- Tolerance for "out-of-the-box" thinking

Slide 13–4

Job of the Brainstorming Leader

- Set and enforce the process rules.
- Manage the group to encourage participation.
- Define the issue so it can be dealt with.
- Keep the discussion on track.
- Record the ideas for later use.

Slide 13–5

Potential Brainstorming Problems

- Group dynamics can get in the way.
- Some members can dominate too much if they are experts or supervisors.
- Criticism can derail the process.
- Some groups are too single-minded.
- It doesn't work as well for decisions with high risk or uncertainty.

Slide 13–6

Common Brainstorming Variations

- Structured brainstorming
- Nominal group technique
- Gordon Technique (reverse brainstorming)
- Brainwriting

Slide 13–7

Using the Brainstorming Ideas

- After the process is completed:
  - Eliminate any truly unworkable ideas.
  - Group similar ideas.
  - Set priority on data gathering and evaluations.
- Decide who (group or individual) does the evaluation.

Slide 13–8

Thoughts About Decision Making

- "Always look for the second right answer— or maybe the third."

  —Anonymous

Slide 13–9

Application Exercise

- Any volunteers to try brainstorming on the decision you listed in module 1? Or on any decision that you need to make now?
- If not, we'll use the worksheet.

Slide 13–10

Checklists and Catalogs

- Checklists can be found anywhere, from textbooks to assembly instructions to *Cosmopolitan* magazine.
- Catalogs include any variation of the term from Office Max to JC Penney; from professional associations to commercial data bases and industrial directories; hard copy or on-line, and so on.

Slide 13–11

Application Exercise

- Any volunteers to discuss what catalogs or checklists might be relevant to the decision you listed in module 1? Or to any decision that you need to make now?
- If not, we'll use the worksheet.

Slide 13–12

Attribute Listing

- Use for physical items (more so than for ideas and concepts).
- Mentally or physically divide an item into its components and consider each part instead of the whole.

Slide 13–13

Exercise

- Any volunteers willing to try attribute listing on the decision you listed in module 1? Or on any decision that you need to make now?
- If not, we'll use the worksheet.

Slide 13–14

Cause-Effect Analysis

- There are several subcategories; we'll cover just two:
  - Fishbone diagrams
  - Matrices (also called Johari windows)
- All are used to find or confirm relationships among facts.

Slide 13–15

Fishbone Diagrams

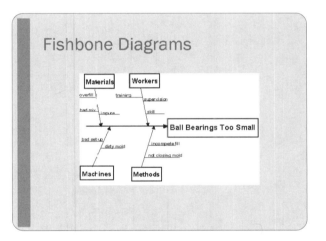

Slide 13–16

Exercise

- Any volunteers willing to try to create a fishbone diagram related to the decision you listed in module 1? Or on any decision that you need to make now?
- If not, we'll use the worksheet.

Slide 13–17

Cause-Effect Matrix Diagrams
(Johari Windows)

	Cause (Female)	Cause does not occur
Effect (like horses)	✓✓✓✓✓✓✓ ✓✓✓✓✓✓✓ ✓✓✓	✓✓✓
Effect does not occur	✓✓	✓✓✓✓✓✓✓ ✓✓✓✓✓✓✓

Slide 13–18

Exercise

- Any volunteers willing to try to create a cause-effect matrix related to the decision you listed in module 1? Or on any decision that you need to make now?
- If not, we'll use the worksheet.

Slide 13–19

Morphological Analysis

- This is more or less the opposite of attribute listing. Instead of taking things apart, you force things together to create new and unexpected combinations.
- This can get out of hand with too many variables, so it needs to be structured, with a minimal number.

Slide 13–20

Exercise

- Any volunteers willing to try doing morphological analysis on the decision you listed in module 1? Or on any decision that you need to make now?
- If not, we'll use the worksheet.

Slide 13–21

Application Exercise

- Use Worksheet 13–7 to work on the decision-making issue you identified in session one of this training program.

Slide 13–22

Review of Module 5

- Describe at least five simple tools that may help improve creativity.
- Apply the appropriate tools to a variety of situations that require creativity.

Slide 13–23

Thank You for Your Attention

- Next meeting:
- Assignment:
- Other announcements?

Slide 13–24

◆

Module 6—The Analytic Process: Narrowing Down the Options

Module 6 focuses on gathering information to make an effective decision. It should be used with programs of a half-day or longer (except the half-day program for managers and supervisors).

Training Objectives

After completing this module, the participants should be able to

* identify significant sources of data for decision-making analysis

* determine the value of collecting additional information

* explain and use the concept of Pareto analysis.

Module 6 Time

* Approximately 1 hour

Note: This schedule includes time for a quick review at the start and a learning check at the end.

Materials

* Attendance list

* Pencils, pens, and paper for each participant

* Whiteboard or flipchart and markers

* Name tags or name tents for each participant

* Worksheet 14–1: Sources of Information

* Computer, screen, and projector for displaying PowerPoint slides; alternatively, overhead projector and overhead transparencies

◆ PowerPoint slide program (slides 14–1 through 14–12)

◆ This chapter for reference or detailed facilitator notes

◆ Optional: music, coffee or other refreshments.

Module Preparation

Arrive ahead of time to greet the participants and make sure materials are available and laid out for the way you want to run the class.

Sample Agenda

0:00   Welcome class.

Have slide 14–1 on the screen as participants arrive.

0:05   PPT presentation.

Begin with slide 14–2 (objectives) and proceed through slide 14–9. See notes on PowerPoint file and in the trainer's notes (below).

0:35   Worksheet.

Distribute Worksheet 14–1: Sources of Information.

Show slide 14–10 as the participants work on worksheet.

Move among participants to keep them on task.

Have the participants discuss answers with others in the class.

0:55   Wrap-up.

Show slide 14–11. Review the objectives with participants.

Ask for questions.

Check for learning (questions can be in oral or printed format).

Show slide 14–12. Dismiss the class.

Trainer's Notes

8:00 a.m. Welcome (5 minutes).

Show slide 14–1 as participants arrive.

Take care of any review and housekeeping items.

8:05 a.m. Gathering Information (15 minutes).

Show slide 14–2 and quickly preview the module topics.

Show slide 14–3. Tell the learners that this section is on gathering information; then provide the following overview: You will usually be aware of the obvious sources of information that will inform your options in decision making. The sources are often unique to the nature of the problem you're trying to solve. The information may be internal to your organization, but sometimes you may need to go to sources outside your department, company, or industry. You will use both primary and secondary data to make your decisions.

Whether internal or external, all information comes from some form of "research." In some cases, you may need to create and collect **primary data**. Primary data comes from basic experimentation. Primary data should be tested, and you must judge performance before you use it. Quality control testing is one example of collecting primary data. So is designing and conducting a survey.

Much of our decision-making information, however, comes from **secondary data**, or data collected by someone else, often for some other purpose, but that is usable for our decision. Examples of secondary data include information from catalogs, census reports, directories, and so on.

For example, for buying a car, we would probably gather both primary and secondary data. For secondary data, we would look up information in publications such as *Consumer Reports* or *Car and Driver*. For primary data, we'd probably visit a showroom for a test drive and to get other sensory perceptions. Obviously the sources we use for the data depend on what we need to know, what's available in secondary sources, how easily and inexpensively we can get it, among other factors.

What do we really need to know in order to make a decision? On most decisions, there will be many pieces of information that we *could* collect. But generally we will want to collect only data that's going to be of use to us.

For example, if you're ready to buy the car, you could check hundreds of things about each option, including fuel tank capacity, length of the windshield-wiper blades, and many other obscure criteria. But why? We want to get only enough information to make a good decision, but not so much as to overwhelm us or cloud the issue.

Experts tell us that one major reason for poor decisions is *too much* data. This is particularly true since the advent of the computer. It's now possible to analyze information easily and report it quickly; however, it may still not all be good information or information we need to make a decision. (Reportedly, one of the major reasons U.S. Defense Intelligence people missed some of the weapons development in North Korea was "data pollution." They had too much information to sort out what they really needed to know. That's often the case, and we must take care to sort out what's really important.)

Secondary data is nearly always cheaper than doing testing on your own. If secondary data is available in a form that applies to your decision, take advantage of it.

If we're buying a new piece of equipment, secondary data sources would include promotional literature from the manufacturer. We expect this to be biased, and if we're looking at several pieces of equipment, the promotional information from each manufacturer might not allow us to make a clear comparison with other products. Perhaps we can find some objective comparison published in a periodical. *Consumer Reports* is a well-known publication that does this, but it only covers merchandise of interest to the general public. This is not much help when we want to compare commercial or industrial equipment options.

Once upon a time, finding information in periodicals meant going to the library and either thumbing through the tables of contents of issues on file or finding the annual index. Today, the search of these references is largely done through hundreds of commercially available online databases and websites that quickly help find information on any topic imaginable. Detailing the use of these resources is beyond the scope of this course. We say that with a note of caution, however, because although the Internet has become an amazing resource for research, it requires skill to separate the fact from the fiction in what we find there. The typical Internet search is confounded by two issues: volume and credibility. Enter a search term or question in most of the search engines and a typical inquiry may come back with thousands of references. Some may be very credible, but others have been posted by the 10-year-old kid down the street. It's not enough to find information on the Internet; you must also be able to verify its accuracy. Most libraries can help you learn how to reach appropriate resources and minimize the volume issue through appropriate searching techniques.

8:20 a.m. How Much Information? (15 minutes).

Show slide 14–4. Point out to the participants that it is impossible to look at every possible car you could buy before you make your choice. Thus, part of the evaluation process is to decide "how much data is enough?"

Sometimes we can determine the exact number of available choices. When this happens, we have a **known population** or **known universe**. Most choices we make come from finite, rather than infinite, populations, but known populations of options can still be quite large.

In some decision-making exercises, we narrow down the population by putting increasingly restrictive limits on our options until we reach a small enough number or narrow enough focus that we can deal with it. In other cases, we may have to remove limits in order to increase the potential choices we have available.

For example, when we're looking for a car to buy, we keep adding (or sometimes dropping) limits until we get to a reasonable number of cars available to consider. We probably start with price and style (sports model or minivan, and so forth), and then we further limit the number available by deciding we'll only buy from certain dealers, and we must have certain options such as an automatic transmission or a cup holder. The effect is to reduce the number of available cars we'll really consider. When we get the population of options down to a manageable number, then we really begin to compare.

Sometimes, though, when we're gathering information for analysis, we can't add limits to the population. For example, if we're checking on quality control, we can't decide to check parts from only one machine. On the other hand, we can't check all parts from all machines, because that would be too time consuming and expensive … and sometimes impossible. Did you hear about the company that went out of business because the boss demanded 100-percent inspection and testing of every ink jet cartridge it produced?

So, when do we have enough information? The answer to this requires us to consider the amount of risk involved in the decision we must make.

Show slide 14–5.

Read the slide to the participants. Malcolm Gladwell, in his bestselling book *Blink*, tells us that even when we try to back up our decisions with research and expert opinion, we can still never be certain we have made the right choice. Most decisions are truly a matter of the "best guess."

Show slide 14–6.

Note: This slide was used before in module 2 (slide 2–10). It is repeated here, and you may choose to use it or not. If participants have seen it recently and understood it, you should delete it or cover it very quickly.

How much risk are you willing to take? Are you a "risk averter" or a "gambler"? A key point in this module is to find ways to reduce the risk. We need to gather information to help us narrow down the options, but what information and how much information? One way to help narrow this down is through the use of Pareto analysis.

Show slide 14–7.

One way to evaluate the importance of a piece of data is a concept called Pareto analysis. Although it's named after a mathematician (Vilfredo Pareto, a 19th-century Italian mathematician and philosopher), it's not really a statistical analysis. You may know of Pareto analysis as "the 80-20 rule" and that it is often used in inventory planning and elsewhere.

Pareto suggests that typically about 80 percent of the activity comes in 20 percent of the participants, whereas about 20 percent of the activity comes in the other 80 percent of the participants.

To demonstrate this, consider the telephone calls you received last year: 80 percent of them may have come from 20 percent of your callers. The other 20 percent of the calls came from the 80 percent of the people who called you once or twice during the year. Is this precisely accurate? Of course not, but the generalized concept is probably true.

How do you spend time in the various rooms in your home? Probably a few rooms make up most of your time; and certain rooms you seldom visit. If you run a grocery store, a large part of your sales comes from a small part of your stock. Milk and bread may make up less than 1 percent of your stock in units or price, but 7 or 8 percent of your sales volume.

Pareto analysis, then, is looking at a collection of data and striving to distinguish the "significant few" from the "trivial many." In this way, you are able to prioritize and focus on areas where your efforts can be most rewarded. For example, if you change phone numbers, notifying just a few key people will mean that most of your calls will be received correctly. If you don't have time to clean the whole house, cleaning only the most used rooms will give you the greatest peace of mind. If you're operating a convenience store, it will matter less if you run out of canned mushrooms than if you run out of two-percent milk, so you'll focus on key needs as you make orders from suppliers.

To use this concept in decision making, just make a list of the data that you could collect, and then reorder that list in the order of each item's importance to your decision.

When you've reordered the list, you'll certainly collect data on the first item or two on the list. As you go down to each subsequent piece of information you might collect, ask yourself how valuable that information is to your decision and how much time and money it will take to collect it. If you predict that it will take a lot of time or cost a lot of money, ask yourself if the additional information will really be that helpful in making a good decision? Will it be cost effective or not? If not, don't collect that information.

Show slide 14–8.

Tell the learners that once they have determined which data is important to have, they must collect and organize it. The organization is essential. For example, it is usually necessary to stratify data into proper groupings. **Stratification** means to divide or sort into two or more meaningful groups that can be examined separately.

If you don't stratify the data, you end up like the audience when a sportscaster came in slightly under the influence one night. He reported the following to his confused audience: "And now, ladies and gentlemen, here are tonight's scores: 37 to 41, 66 to 12, 39 to 22, 18 to 44, and, in a big upset, 52 to 33!" You know *something*, but it's not all that clear or useful. The names of the teams and which sport he's discussing would be helpful to know.

Stratification makes irregularities or relationships more readily stand out. It is, therefore, an essential aid to problem solving and decision making.

For example, if you're gathering data to be used for quality control, and you have several possible sources of poor-quality production, be certain you can trace any problem to its cause. This may mean collecting data separately from each machine or each worker or each supplier. This will reduce difficulties during the problem-solving stage.

When you have a small population of options, you may want to get information on all of them. For example, if you're trying to decide which among five computer systems to buy, you should get details on each.

Let's say you want information on how your customers would react to a change in your product design. If you only have a few customers, you might ask them all. If you have thousands of customers, though, you'll never get all of their opinions. If you did, it would be very expensive and time consuming.

For a large population, you can get reasonably reliable information by selecting a small, appropriate sample amount of that population to examine. **Sampling** is widely accepted in our culture in things such as TV Arbitron ratings, political polls, or free samples of food given in grocery stores. In a later session, we will present information on sampling techniques.

Show slide 14–9.

Read the John D. Turner quote and discuss its meaning with the class.

8:35 a.m. Application Exercise (20 minutes).

Show slide 14–10. Distribute Worksheet 14-1: Sources of Information.

Worksheet Instructions. This is the sixth worksheet in the series. Ask the trainees to reconsider the decision or problem they listed in the pretest and have been working with in each module so far. For that problem or decision, ask them to list what information they need to collect to make the decision. Then have them apply Pareto's principle to the list, to choose the pieces of information that are most critical. Finally, ask the participants to make a list explaining how they intend to go about collecting the information. This may be a list of sources (individuals, records, websites, and so forth) or an explanation of a primary data collection process they will use. As in previous modules, participants may work individually or in groups.

8:55 a.m. Module 6 Summary (5 minutes).

Show slide 14–11. Review the key points of the module and use the learning check questions below as either an oral or printed learning check.

LEARNING CHECK QUESTIONS

You can use the learning check questions and answers in oral or printed form.

Discussion Questions

  ◆ Define primary and secondary data

    Answer: See slide 14–3.

◆ What is the most practical way to use Pareto analysis?

Answer: First, list the information you could collect to help make a decision and then order it from most to least important.

◆ List potential sources of primary and secondary information for a decision whether to move your company offices to another nearby city.

Answer: Primary information could include surveys of employees and customers, internal financial information, and so forth. *Secondary information* could include government information on the economy and labor market, real estate information, tax incentives available, quality-of-life surveys, and so forth.

◆ In the next month, your company must develop its first-ever product catalog. How would Pareto analysis apply to this action?

Answer: Pareto analysis would help you focus on separating the significant few products from the trivial many, to focus attention on your key products.

Multiple Choice Questions

1. Vilfredo Pareto is known for his contribution to

   a. Creativity theory

   b. Problem-solving technique

   c. Analysis of priorities *(answer)*

   d. Pasta sauce ingredients

2. Decision-making information found in a product review in *Consumer Reports* is always an example of _____ information.

   a. Quantitative

   b. Qualitative

   c. Secondary *(answer)*

   d. Primary

9:00 a.m. Thank You for Your Attention.

Show slide 14–12 . Edit the slide to present information relevant to your class.

Worksheet 14–1
Sources of Information

Instructions: Use this worksheet to identify sources of information to help you make your decision.

What primary or secondary sources of information are available to help you make this decision (people, records, documents, websites or other data sources, articles, books, consultants, and so forth)?

◆ _____

◆ _____

◆ _____

◆ _____

◆ _____

Plan for collecting the information.

How will you collect the information you need?

_____

_____

_____

_____

_____

MAKING EFFECTIVE DECISIONS

Module 6
Narrowing Down the Options

Slide 14–1

Module 6 Topics

- Identify significant sources of data for decision-making analysis.
- Determine the value of collecting additional information.
- Explain and use the concept of Pareto analysis.

Slide 14–2

Gathering Information

- Sources of primary data
  - Getting unique information that has not been collected before.
- Sources of secondary data
  - Usable data collected for another purpose and probably by someone else.

Slide 14–3

How Much Information?

- How many options are there?
  - A couple or an infinite number?
- How difficult or expensive is it to obtain?
- How much risk is associated with the decision?

Slide 14–4

Thoughts About Decision Making

- We like market research because it provides "certainty"—a score, a prediction. If someone asks us why we made the decision we did, we can point to a number. But the truth is that for the most important decisions, there can be no certainty.

  —Malcolm Gladwell

Slide 14–5

Risk in Decisions

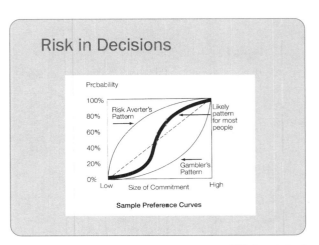

Sample Preference Curves

Slide 14–6

Pareto Analysis

Pareto analysis is a technique to separate the significant few from the trivial many.

- Also known as the "80-20 rule"
- In inventory, it's called "ABC analysis."

Slide 14–7

Organizing the Data

- To help you make a decision, data must be organized into meaningful groups.
- Separate necessary from nice-to-have data.
- If collecting primary data, consider sampling techniques.

Slide 14–8

Thoughts About Decision Making

- "Too often, our minds are locked on one track. We are looking for red — so we overlook blue. Many Nobel Prizes have been washed down the drain because someone did not expect the unexpected."
  — John D. Turner

Slide 14–9

Application Exercise

- Complete Worksheet 14-1 and discuss it with others in the group.

Slide 14–10

Module 6 Review

- Identify significant sources of data for decision-making analysis.
- Determine the value of collecting additional information.
- Explain and use the concept of Pareto analysis.

Slide 14–11

Thank You for Your Attention

- Next meeting:
- Assignment:
- Other announcements?

Slide 14–12

Module 7—Using Everyday Statistics

Module 7 covers some very basic concepts of statistics that may be helpful when making decisions. It should be used with the multiple-day program schedules. *Special suggestion with this module*: If your boss is going to walk by the training room and see people playing with cards and dice, perhaps you should first warn him or her about the relevance of the exercise.

Training Objectives

After completing this module, the participants should be able to

- define probability, using everyday examples

- use the concept of probability to explain gambling situations

- explain the process and uses of sampling data related to decision making.

Module 7 Time

- Approximately 1.5 hours

Note: This schedule includes time for a quick review at the start and a learning check at the end.

Materials

- Attendance list

- Pencils, pens, and paper for each participant

- Whiteboard or flipchart and markers

- Name tags or name tents for each participant

- Worksheet 15–1: Probability, Combinations, and Permutations

- ◆ Worksheet 15–2: Statistical Techniques

- ◆ Computer, screen, and projector for displaying PowerPoint slides; alternatively, overhead projector and overhead transparencies

- ◆ PowerPoint slide program (slides 15–1 through 15–23)

- ◆ This chapter for reference or detailed facilitator notes

- ◆ Optional: music, coffee, or other refreshments. Also, having calculators available for participants will be useful (one per subgroup or one per participant).

- ◆ Several decks of cards and several pairs of dice.

Module Preparation

Arrive ahead of time to greet the participants and make sure materials are available and laid out for the way you want to run the class. Turn on and test computer equipment.

NOTE ABOUT THIS MODULE: MAKE IT FUN

This module can be intimidating to many participants (and to a few trainers). But the worksheets, PowerPoint slides, and trainer's notes will encourage you to make this module fun by drawing on the intuitive understanding that people have about statistics (though they might not have brought it to the conscious surface previously).

Observe the skill levels and levels of comfort of your participants and adjust your presentation accordingly. This session should not be lecture-only. For the exercises, you may want to ease any pressure by mixing groups with skilled and unskilled people and by demonstrating steps on the whiteboard or flipchart item by item.

Work on the concepts one at a time (that's how the slides are designed). Rather than presenting the concepts as a solid block, insert the slides with quotes and promote discussion between the concepts. You may also want to split up the worksheet into several parts and give out one problem at a time.

Sample Agenda

0:00   Welcome the class.

Have slide 15–1 on the screen as participants arrive.

0:05 Exercise.

Hand out the card decks and dice, and suggest that people discuss gambling.

0:20 PPT Presentation and worksheets.

Begin with slide 15–2 (objectives) and proceed through slide 15–21. See notes in the PowerPoint file and in the Trainer's Notes. Distribute Worksheet 15–1: Probability, Combinations, and Permutations.

See notes below on preparation of worksheets for this module.

Move among participants to keep them on task.

It's OK for participants to discuss answers with others.

1:15 Practice.

Continue work on Worksheet 15–1: Probability, Combinations, and Permutations and distribute Worksheet 15–2: Statistical Techniques.

1:25 Wrap-up.

Show slide 15–22. Review the module 7 objectives with the class.

Ask for questions and concerns.

Check for learning (questions can be in oral or printed format).

Show slide 15–23. Dismiss the class.

Trainer's Notes

8:00 a.m. Welcome (10 minutes).

Show slide 15–1 as participants arrive.

Take care of housekeeping items.

Distribute card decks and dice. Encourage the participants to talk among themselves about the idea of gambling.

8:10 a.m. Probability (40 minutes).

Show slide 15–2 and preview module 7 topics.

Note: This module is designed so that the worksheet exercises are intermixed with the PowerPoint presentation. Allow about 50 to 60 minutes to complete slides 15–2 through 15–19. You can also include an optional short (5-minute) break at a convenient point during that time. If you prefer to do all of the worksheet exercises at the end, you'll need to adjust the PowerPoint slides accordingly and not distribute the worksheets until you've completed slide 15–21.

Show slide 15–3. Go over the probability examples on the slide with the participants or have them work alone on the calculations.

Show slide 15–4.

Go over the answers with the class. The first two are pretty easy, but you may want to illustrate the third. Go to the board and write out the calculation. Using two different color markers (red and black, for example), write out two columns of numbers: one through six, one red column and one black column. Then match up the numbers in the red column and the black column that add to seven. Circle the combinations that add to seven: R1/B6; R2/B5; R3/B4; R4/B3; R5/B2; R6/B1. Six different combinations add up to seven and 30 combinations don't. So the odds of rolling a seven are six to 30, or one to five.

Ask the learners why the final (the rain forecast) example is different.

Explain that the last example is different because there are other unknown factors at work. The probability for rain is based on a computer model, probably using artificial intelligence software, which takes the atmospheric conditions projected for the next day and manipulates it to compare with similar conditions in the past and how often it rained under those conditions. Or, in the small towns it may be that six out of 10 of the guys at Mel's coffee shop have back pain, so it works out at 60 percent chance of rain.

Show slide 15–5, and discuss how the past is not a true predictor of the future.

Show slide 15–6. In addition to reading the text of the slide, explain the concept of an exponent. $(1/2)^3$ means that the number (one-half in this case) multiplied by itself the number of times shown in the exponent (three, in this case). So $1/2 \times 1/2 \times 1/2 = 1/8$.

 Show slide 15–7.

Allow a minute or two for the participants to answer the three questions on the slide. The answers to the questions:

(1) $1/6 \times 1/6 \times 1/6 = 1/216$ or odds of 216 to one.

(2) Drawing from three decks would be calculated as $(4/52)^3 = 4/52 \times 4/52 \times 4/52 =$ one out of 2,197.

(3) Drawing three aces from one deck (without replacing the card drawn) would be calculated as 4/52 × 3/51 × 2/50 = 0.000181 or about 1 out of 5525.

Show slide 15–8. This slide will be self-explanatory for many participants, but be prepared to explain "mutually exclusive." And be prepared to explain "4/52 + 26/52 − 2/52 = 28/52." Four out of 52 cards are aces, 26 out of 52 cards are red, and two cards are red aces, so those two have been double counted and therefore two needs to be subtracted. They are not mutually exclusive because a card can be both red and an ace.

Show slide 15–9. Distribute Worksheet 15–1: Probability, Combinations, and Permutations. Allow no more than five minutes for the first part of the worksheet.

Now, you have choices to make about how you present the next exercises.

1. Either allow participants to work together, or change the slide if you don't want them to work together.

2. Present all the questions on the worksheet at once, or split up the worksheet and distribute the parts as you go along.

After distributing Worksheet 15–1, allow time for participants to solve the first question: (1) What are the odds of getting four heads and no tails out of flipping four coins? Then show the next slide.

Show slide 15–10.

Discuss the quote with the participants.

Direct participants to answer the second question on Worksheet 15–1. (2) What is the probability of drawing an ace and a black king on two consecutive draws from the same deck without replacing cards?

After allowing time for participants to calculate the answer, put the answer on the whiteboard or flipchart.

On the first draw, chances are four out of 52 that you will draw an ace; on the second draw, your chances are two out of 51 that you will draw a black king. Therefore, your chances of drawing an ace and a black king in two draws is the product of those two multiplied, or (4/52) × (2/51) = 2/663.

Show slide 15–11.

Explain the "!" notation in math. This is called "factorial" and means any integer multiplied by each integer less than itself. So, 4! = 4 × 3 × 2 × 1 = 24.

Be prepared to discuss why order of selection is not important for combinations and why it is important in calculating permutations.

Show slide 15–12.

Direct participants to answer the third question on Worksheet 15–1. (3) Five different color balls are in a box. If you draw out three at random, how many different combinations can be created?

After allowing time for participants to calculate the answer, put the answer on the board or flipchart.

$$(5!) \div (3!)(5 - 3)! = (5 \times 4 \times 3 \times 2 \times 1) \div (3 \times 2 \times 1)(2 \times 1) = 120 \div 12 = 10$$

Show slide 15–13. Review the material on the slide.

Show slide 15–14.

Direct participants to answer the fourth question on the Worksheet 15–1: (4) How many different ways can you sequence the words "love," "honor," and "obey"?).

After allowing time for participants to calculate the answer, put the answer on the whiteboard or flipchart.

$$3! \div 1! = (3 \times 2 \times 1) \div (1) = 6$$

love, honor, obey

love, obey, honor

honor, love, obey

honor, obey, love

obey, love, honor

obey, honor, love

Show slide 15–15. Read the slide or let the participants read it. It shows additional ways that these principles can be applied.

Show slide 15–16. This John McEnroe quote is just to get a smile and reduce some of the tension that working with statistics usually causes.

8:50 a.m. Break (Optional) (5 minutes).

Usually people need one by now. Keep it short.

8:55 a.m. Data Sampling (20 minutes).

Show slide 15–17.

Explain that the next section is about data sampling. We don't have time for a comprehensive treatment of the subject of sampling. Like the rest of this training program, we hope that you'll use sampling as a tool for gathering data to help with your decision-making process when it's appropriate. If any of you actually needs to design a sampling study, you should contact someone who understands it in greater depth than provided here.

We see sampling results in the news every day from political polls. For years, *USA Today* has featured the results of sampling and polling. Somewhere in your organization at this moment, there is sampling taking place. Where is that likely to be? (Quality control and marketing are likely answers.) *Note:* See if you can find some recent relevant examples to use - political polls or other polls show up almost every day in newspapers. There may also be some from your company experience.

We'll discuss how many samples you need to become reasonably certain of accuracy. The size of the sample should be determined by the nature of what you're sampling. In the grocery store, you may only need one taste of Harry's Horribly Hot Jalapeno Dip to decide whether or not you want to buy it. On the other hand, Harry probably needs to sample quite a few cans of his production to ensure that the quality is staying where he wants it. He also needs to sample a number of customers to see if the recipe needs to be changed. He probably should not change it based on just one person's opinion.

Show slide 15–18.

Introduce the concept of sampling. For sampling to be useful, it must truly represent the entire population from which it is taken. For example, a poll to determine political attitudes of the country could not be conducted only in Boston or only in San Diego. To ensure the representativeness of a sample, you must first know something about the population.

Populations that are truly homogeneous can be sampled in any manner. Probably very few truly homogeneous populations exist, but there are many in which the differences are not significant or not related to the variable being measured. **Random samples** can be taken at any time, any place, in any order. All that's necessary is to get a sufficient quantity of samples.

In many cases, however, **stratified samples** are necessary. To stratify means to ensure that there is a representative mix of the population within the sample. Let's use an example: if you're sampling a production process, you need to sample across all time periods and job categories. If you sampled only mornings or materials handlers, your information would only be usable for that group at that time.

Common categories (or variables) for stratification include

Time. Commonly, an equal number of samples is taken each hour of operation.

Location. All locations of operation should be appropriately represented in the sample.

Machine. Products made on various machines need to be included in the sample to ensure overall accuracy.

Worker. Work done by each worker needs to be included in the sample.

Demographic data. Public opinion surveys need to include representative mixes of various ages, races, employment categories, income levels, and so forth.

Other factors. Any categories that could potentially provide different data than the rest of the sample need to be proportionately included.

You can determine through statistical means how accurately and with what level of confidence a sample represents its population. An easy-to-remember number, which is a standard in the sampling business, is 1111. That's the largest number of samples you'll ever need to take out of a population to be 98 percent certain that your sample is within plus or minus 3 percent of the actual population. Depending on what you're sampling, you may need dramatically fewer samples. Sampling theory is the subject of entire text-books. The only concern we have is to explain how many samples are needed to reach a given level of accuracy. In general, the more samples (properly taken samples, at least), the greater the accuracy. The level of accuracy is expressed in terms of plus or minus a certain percent accuracy at a specific level of confidence. For example, we might be 98 percent confident that our sample is plus or minus 3 percent accurate.

The first number is a probability (98 percent of the time under these conditions), and the other is a statement of relativity (the figures we have developed from our sample are within 3 percent of the actual population). The two terms work in tandem. Probability will increase (get higher) as the variation from population increases. For certain samples, it might be equally true to say that we are 95 percent confident of plus or minus 3 percent accuracy, or that we are 99 percent confident of plus or minus 10 percent accuracy.

You must start with the confidence level you wish to have. 90, 95, 98, and 99 percent are common choices in statistics. Given that confidence level, you determine the accuracy level based on the number of samples and the ratio of the samples in the largest category to the total samples. The table on the next slide indicates the samples needed for 3 percent accuracy at 98 percent confidence.

Show slide 15–19.

9:15 a.m. Application Exercise (10 minutes).

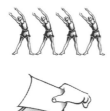

Show slide 15–20. Distribute Worksheet 15–2: Statistical Techniques and allow participants to complete it. Move among them to keep them on task. This worksheet continues the pattern of building on decisions identified in module 1.

Show slide 15–21.

Review the Lovin' Spoonful quote with the class. Have a sing-along, if you wish. If you're using music with your lesson design, this song might be a good choice.

9:25 a.m. Module 7 Summary (5 minutes).

Show slide 15–22, and review the key points of the module. Use the following questions, as desired.

LEARNING CHECK QUESTIONS

You can use the learning check questions and answers in oral or printed form.

Discusssion Questions

- ◆ Does an honest deck of cards represent a known or an unknown universe?

  Answer: a known universe

- ◆ Why is sampling a good idea in collection of information?

  Answer: It's usually cheaper and faster than polling the entire population, especially if you have an unknown population or large known population of possibilities.

♦ What steps can improve the accuracy of the results of a survey to collect primary data on product preference?

Answer: (1) Increase the number of samples, (2) ensure the sample is properly stratified to reflect the target population and (3) pretest questions for reliability and validity.

♦ A legal game at the county fair allows you to put $1 on a number, spin a wheel with 20 numbers on it, and win $10 if the wheel stops at your number. List and explain three or four things that would influence your decision whether or not to play this game.

Possible answers: (1) your attitude toward gambling, (2) your need for $1 (can I afford to lose it?), (3) your tolerance for risk, and (4) the odds of winning, and so forth.

Multiple Choice Questions

1. The best example of probability that involves a *known universe* is

   a. Predicting which candidate will win the election

   b. Playing a game of poker *(answer)*

   c. Guessing the number of beans in a jar

   d. Buying a used car that won't break down.

2. Which of the numbers below is more likely than others to result from a single roll of a pair of fair dice?

   a. 2

   b. 6 *(answer)*

   c. 10

   d. 12

9:30 a.m. Thank You for Your Attention.

Show slide 15–23. Edit slide to show relevant information.

Worksheet 15–1

Probability, Combinations, and Permutations

Calculate the following probabilities:

1. What are the odds of getting four heads and no tails out of flipping four coins?

2. What is the probability of drawing an ace and a black king on two draws from the same deck (without replacing cards)?

Calculate the following combination:

3. Five different color balls are in a box. If you draw out three at random, how many different combinations can be created?

Calculate the following permutation:

4. How many ways can sequence the words "love," "honor," and "obey"?

Answers (*Note:* Do not print the answers on the same page as the questions.)

$(1/2)^4 = 1/16$ or one out of sixteen

HHHH, HHHT, HHTT, HTTT

HHTT, HHTH, HTHH, HTHT

THHH, THHT, THTT, TTTT

TTHH, TTTH, THTT, THTH

First-draw chances are four out of 52; second-draw chances are two out of 51. Therefore the total chance is the product of those two multiplied, or $(4/52) \times (2/51) = 2/663$

$(5!) \div (3!)(5 - 3)! = (5 \times 4 \times 3 \times 2 \times 1) \div (3 \times 2 \times 1)(2 \times 1) = 10$

$3! \div 1! = (3 \times 2 \times 1) \div (1) = 6$

love, honor, obey

love, obey, honor

honor, love, obey

honor, obey, love

obey, love, honor

obey, honor, love

Worksheet 15–2
Statistical Techniques

Restate the decision that you are working on for this training program.

_____

What data is required to treat your decision with statistics?

◆   _____

◆   _____

◆   _____

◆   _____

◆   _____

What sampling data might be collected and how would you collect it?

_____

_____

_____

Will random samples do, or do you need to stratify the data in any way? If so, how?

_____

_____

MAKING EFFECTIVE DECISIONS

Module 7
Everyday Uses of Statistics

Slide 15–1

Module 7 Topics

- Define probability using common examples.
- Use the concept of probability to explain common simple decision-making situations.
- Explain the process and uses of sampling data related to decision making.

Slide 15–2

Examples of "Probability"

- Chance of heads in a single coin flip
- Chance of pulling an ace out of a card deck
- Chance of rolling a 7 with a pair of dice
- Chance of rain tomorrow ??

Slide 15–3

Known vs. Unknown

- Coin flip is simple: 50-50 (with a fair coin)
- 4 Aces in a deck of 52 cards (no jokers) means a 4 in 52 chance of an ace (~7.7%)
- Dice can land 36 different ways; 6 of these add up to 7 (about a 17% chance)
- Rain – how is that number generated?

  Sometimes all the possible outcomes aren't known.

Slide 15–4

"Gambler's Fallacy"

- The belief that prior events influence future events in a purely random situation.

  For example, thinking that having gotten 3 heads in a row increases the chance of getting a tails next time. It doesn't. It's still 50-50!

Slide 15–5

Multiple Probabilities

- Possible outcomes of two coin flips are:
  - TT, HT, TH, and HH, so the odds of two heads or two tails are 1 out of 4.
- Possible outcomes of three coin flips are:
  - TTT, TTH, THT, THH, HTT, HTH, HHT, and HHH, so the odds of three heads or three tails are 1 out of 8.
- The formula: (odds of each)$^{\text{number of flips}}$ or $(\frac{1}{2})^3$

Slide 15–6

Application Exercise

- What are the odds of getting three *1*'s by rolling three dice?
- What are the odds of getting three aces by drawing one card from each of three decks?
- Why would it be different than drawing three cards from one deck?

Slide 15–7

Cumulative Probabilities

- The odds of drawing an ace <u>or</u> a king?
  - They're mutually exclusive, so just add the odds of each: 4/52 plus 4/52 = 8/52
- The odds of drawing an ace or a red card?
  - They're not mutually exclusive, so add them, then subtract the overlap:
    4/52 plus 26/52 minus 2/52 = 28/52

Slide 15–8

Application Exercise

- Complete the first part of the worksheet. Have your friends help you out, if necessary.

Slide 15–9

Thoughts About Decision Making

- "Acquisition of facts does not constitute knowledge."

  —Anonymous

Slide 15–10

Combinations and Permutations

- **Combinations**: Order of selection is not important. For example: Eight swimmers are in a race for three slots in the Olympics; how many combinations of 3 swimmers can advance? Answer: 56 possible combinations

$$\frac{8!}{(3!) \times (8-3)!} = \frac{8 \times 7 \times 6 \times 5 \times 4 \times 3 \times 2 \times 1}{(3 \times 2 \times 1)(5 \times 4 \times 3 \times 2 \times 1)} = \frac{40320}{720} = 56$$

Slide 15–11

Application Exercise

- Complete the next part of the worksheet. Have your friends help you out, if necessary.

Slide 15–12

Combinations and Permutations

- Permutations: Order of selection is important. For example, in the same set of swimmers as before, how many possible permutations are there for eight people to finish first, second, and third? Answer: 336

$$\frac{8!}{5!} = \frac{8\times7\times6\times5\times4\times3\times2\times1}{5\times4\times3\times2\times1} = 336$$

Slide 15–13

Application Exercise

- Complete the last part of the worksheet. Have your friends help you out, if necessary.

Slide 15–14

Combinations and Permutations

- You have six dinner guests. How many different ways can you seat them around a table? Answer: $6! \div 1! = 720$. Amazing!
- Your state lottery is based on 6 numbers out of a possible 1 to 47. What are the odds of getting all 6? Answer: $(47!) \div (6! \times 41!) =$ one chance out of 10,737,573.

Slide 15–15

Thoughts About Decision Making

- "This taught me a lesson, but I'm not sure what it is."

    —John McEnroe, on losing to Tim Mayotte in the U.S. Pro Indoor Championships

Slide 15–16

Sampling Data

- Most decisions can't be based on 100 percent information. Sampling is a common technique in many business operations such as quality control, marketing, political polling, and even food samples in a grocery store.

Slide 15–17

Sampling Data

- Random vs. stratified
    - Time, location, machine, worker, demographic data, etc., can be used for stratification.
- "Confidence" and "Accuracy" levels
    - Confidence is expressed as a probability percentage; 90%, 95%, 98% & 99% are common.
    - Accuracy is expressed as a relative plus or minus percentage; 1%, 2% & 3% are common.

Slide 15–18

Sampling Data

If the largest category in the sample is:	5% or 95%	10% or 90%	20% or 80%	25% or 75%	40% or 60%	50%
You need this many samples to be 98% certain of estimations +/- 3% accurate.	211	400	711	833	1067	1111

Slide 15–19

Application Exercise

- Complete the second worksheet, which applies the material from this module to the decision you identified during the first module.

Slide 15–20

Thoughts About Decision Making

- ♫ ♫ "Did you ever have to make up your mind? Say 'yes' to one and leave the other behind? It's not often easy; it's not often kind. Did you ever have to make up your mind?" ♫ ♫

  — The Lovin' Spoonful

Slide 15–21

Review

- Define *probability* using common examples.
- Use the concept of *probability* to explain common simple decision making situations.
- Explain the process and uses of sampling data related to decision making.

Slide 15–22

Thank You for Your Attention

- Next meeting:
- Assignment:
- Other announcements?

Slide 15–23

Module 8—Using Tools to Improve Analysis

Module 8 covers very simple tools that may be helpful when making decisions.

Training Objectives

After completing this module, the participants should be able to

- describe at least five simple tools that may help improve analysis of information

- apply the appropriate tools to a variety of situations requiring analysis of information.

Module 8 Time

- Approximately 2 hours

Note: This schedule includes time for a quick review at the start and a learning check at the end and includes time for a 10-minute break.

Materials

- Attendance list

- Pencils, pens, and paper for each participant

- Whiteboard or flipchart, and markers

- Name tags or name tents for each participant

- Worksheet 16–1: Decision Matrix Worksheet

- Worksheet 16–2: Decomposition Trees, Decision Trees, and Scatter Diagrams (optional)

- Worksheet 16–3: Value-Matrix Template

◆ Worksheet 16–4: Reviewing Your Decisions So Far

◆ Computer, screen, and projector for displaying PowerPoint slides; alternatively overhead projector and overhead transparencies

◆ PowerPoint slide program (slides 16–1 through 16–16)

◆ Software and files

◆ This chapter for reference or detailed trainer's notes

◆ Optional: music, coffee, or other refreshments

◆ Also, having calculators available will be useful (have either one per subgroup or one per participant).

Module Preparation

Arrive ahead of time to greet the participants and make sure materials are available and laid out for the way you want to run the class. Turn on and test the computer equipment.

SUGGESTIONS FOR THIS MODULE

This module can be intimidating to many participants and some instructors.

You should observe the skill levels and levels of comfort of your participants and adjust your presentation accordingly. This module should not be lecture only. You can ease the pressure on individual participants by mixing groups with skilled and unskilled people and by doing the calculations on the whiteboard or flipchart.

The worksheets are designed to cover the material whether presented together at the end of the session or presented one at a time as the concepts are introduced. There are two reasons for this: First, the final worksheet does not require everyone to work on each tool that's covered. Second, many participants may find the tools slow to design and develop, in which case the timing would be difficult to control in a training setting.

Sample Agenda

0:00   Welcome the class.

Have slide 16–1 up on the screen as participants arrive.

0:05   PowerPoint presentation, with discussion.

         Move through slides 16–2 to 16–9, discussing and demonstrating each concept. You will probably need to use flipcharts or a whiteboard for some of this.

0:55   Break.

1:05   PowerPoint presentation with discussion.

         Move through slides 16–10 to 16–13, discussing and demonstrating each concept.

1:25   Practice worksheets.

         For Worksheets 16–1 and 16–4, ask participants to use one of the decisions they identified on the pretest at the start of the course.

         You may also present Worksheets 16–2 and 16–3, as time allows.

         See the directions with slide 16–14.

1:55   Wrap-up.

         Use slide 16–15 to review module 8.

         Ask for questions and make any further assignments.

2:00   Use slide 16–16 to dismiss the class. Edit the slide, so it contains appropriate information.

Trainer's Notes

8:00 a.m. Welcome (5 minutes).

Show slide 16–1 as participants arrive.

Take care of housekeeping items.

8:05 a.m. Decision Matrix (15 minutes).

Show slide 16–2 and preview the objectives. Tell the participants that now you will cover decision matrices. A decision matrix is a deductive tool for general decision making among options of various types. The overall purpose of using a decision matrix is to provide a structure to comparing options that may not be directly comparable, due to their complexity. A matrix discipline forces you to consider each option, one criterion at a time, therefore structuring your thoughts rationally instead of leaving them confused with the problem. Without a matrix, each option has both some good and some bad points, and therefore no clear choice emerges.

Typical decisions that might be aided by a decision matrix include where to go on vacation, which new car to buy, where to open up a branch office, which applicant to hire for a job opening, or any other decision among complex alternatives.

The decision matrix can be developed in several forms. We will introduce them from the simplest to more complex. The first type of decision matrix is extremely simple, employing only a "yes or no" judgment. They get more complex as you add scaling, then weighting and scaling, to the process.

Show slide 16–3. You are trying to decide where to take a family vacation. You have narrowed it to four possible options: the mountains, the seashore, an overseas site, or a big city. Using the simplest matrix, you might begin by listing what your family is looking for in the vacation (fresh air, entertainment, and so on). Your matrix might look like the one on slide 16–3. Based on this, your choice would be to go to the mountains because it received the greatest number of check marks. Note, also, that because all four options received check marks under "entertainment for spouse and me," that particular criterion had no effect on the outcome and could have been eliminated.

Your next step could be adding some numbers to sharpen the decision making, using a scale of one to five to measure the relative importance of factors such as cost and travel time.

Show slide 16–4. Your decision matrix can be more complex by adding a scale. Let's return to our vacation example: Your list of desired qualities are cost, travel time required, relaxation expected, ease of travel to the site, and family fun—each ranked on a scale of one to five.

Let's assume your thought process goes like this:

> *Mountains:* Low cost gives mountains a five out of five, but the long drive gives mountains only a two out of five. It'll be relaxing when you get there, so that's another five out of five. Driving to the mountains doesn't require a passport or other complications, so it gets another five. On the other hand, your kids hate the idea, which brings the mark for "family fun" down to a one.

> *Note:* Present the rankings of the other three choices in a similar fashion.

> *Seashore:* More expensive than the mountains, but closer. It, too, will be relaxing. Drive goes through big cities. Kids approve; spouse is ambivalent.

Overseas: Expensive, but flying is quick. Tough to relax in unfamiliar surroundings. Need passport, different money, interpreter, and guide. Sounds like fun to the family.

Big city: Expensive, short drive, hectic, but not too complex. Lots of museums and excitement.

After all that, you still don't have a clear winner because the mountains and seashore columns have equal scores. But you might at least eliminate two of the options (overseas and big city), then go back and add some other criteria—or just flip a coin.

Or you could move on to a better way of ranking, by assigning relative weights to the importance of each of the five criteria in your matrix.

Show slide 16–5 and introduce example three, the Weighted Decision Matrix. In all probability, your criteria are not of equal importance to you. The matrix shown adds a criterion weighting scale of 1 to 10. This gives cost the major impact on the decision, with ease of travel and relaxation as the two least important criteria.

Other than the weighting column, the rest of the numbers are the same as the previous slide. To get the weighted score, you multiply the number in each cell by the number in the weight column. This is shown by the numbers in the parentheses. Then you add each column. So for the mountains, your rating was a five out of five for cost (meaning it's the cheapest, because a low cost would be rated the best). Multiply that five by the nine (out of 10) that you're weighting the cost, and you get 45. Do the same for each cell in the matrix and add the scores at the bottom.

Your preference would be for the choice that received the greatest number of points, so this would eliminate an overseas or big city vacation. In this case, a trip to the mountains is best and the seashore a close second.

Now we move to a tool designed to help determine the "expected value" of a transaction. Expected values are index numbers useful as a basis for comparison of alternatives. The expected-value computation uses a combination of the decision matrix and probabilities.

The basic difference between this new tool and the decision matrices on the previous slides is that in the earlier matrices we used *relative* scales (such as one to five) to evaluate each criterion, whereas entries in the next step, the expected-value matrix, are *real numbers* representing actual or projected outcomes from each alternative under the various conditions.

8:20 a.m. Expected-Value Matrices (10 minutes).

Show slide 16–6. Refer to the top graph (Unweighted Expected-Value Matrix). This example shows an expected-value matrix for someone who has money to invest and has a choice of three different investment policies suggested by her financial advisor. These three investment policies will perform differently, depending on whether we have a period of inflation, recession, or depression in the economy.

To create an expected-value matrix, the decision maker must know: (1) the alternatives available (rows A, B, and C—think of them as alternative investment portfolios, with different rates of return), (2) the likely conditions under which these alternatives will be operating (the columns: inflation, depression, and recession), and (3) the predicted result for each alternative under each condition (to be entered in the expected value column). For quick comparison of the three alternatives, we record the average expected values of each alternative investment portfolios in the expected-value column.

In the example on the screen, for each $100 invested, Option A will earn $16 a year if there is inflation, $11 a year if there is a depression, and $6 a year if there is a recession. Option B earns $8, $11, and loses $1 under each condition. The expected value is essentially an estimate of what would happen if you made these investments over and over and over. In the long run, if all three conditions occurred approximately an equal number of times, Option A would earn an average of $11 a year for each $100 invested; Option B would earn $6; and Option C would earn $9.

But then we realize that inflation, depression, and recession are not equally probable. To take that into account, we predict the probabilities of each of those conditions and weight the expected values accordingly.

Refer to the bottom graph (Weighted Expected-Value Matrix): With recession as the most likely condition (70 percent), rows A and C become equally preferred alternatives.

Computing the expected value of alternative courses of action provides a rational basis for comparison of each to the other. Although the actual outcome is unlikely to be exactly as computed, a relative likelihood of profit or value can be established among the alternatives under various conditions. The result of the computation is an index number for each alternative.

Recap: Step-by-Step Instructions for Creating an Expected-Value Matrix

Step 1: List vertically the various options being considered.

Step 2: List horizontally across the top the various conditions that might occur to affect the outcome.

Step 3: Determine what the result is likely to be for each of the options under each of the conditions specified. Enter this index number in the appropriate spot in the matrix.

Step 4a: If the conditions are equally likely, compute the expected value by just taking the average of the rates for each of the options.

Step 4b: If the conditions are not equally likely, this changes the analysis. Predict the likelihood of each condition, and then compute the expected value by weighting the table in a manner similar to that described for the decision matrix.

Depending on your time and interest, here are some optional questions that will help to bring home the idea of a weighted expected value matrix. They will add about five minutes to the presentation. Questions that might occur to the investor at this point include:

◆ How much would additional information about the portfolios be worth in deciding where to invest?

◆ How much would you pay another expert for an opinion?

◆ What action might ensure that one investment outperformed the others?

An investor who knew it was going to be inflation would certainly choose Policy A over Policy C. What do you think? He or she might choose A anyway (50/50 chance). Is it worth $5 per $100 to know what it'll be?

8:30 a.m. Decomposition Trees (20 minutes).

Show slide 16–7. Provide the participants an overview of decomposition trees. Decomposition trees are a visual aid for understanding the parts that make up a whole. The trees look like traditional organization charts. Their purpose is to help in the "decomposition" or breaking up a larger item into its components. They could be used for a variety of decision-making or problem-solving needs, such as to analyze a budget, review staffing in an organization, or help with a job analysis by a human resources specialist to determine which tasks an individual performs in a job. The results might also be used in the development of a Pareto analysis.

Refer to slide 16–7 as you go over the following example. As part of the data collection to plan for the company's budget for next year, you have decided to use a decomposition tree to display the current budget. You break down the current budget allocations according to your organization's structure. Note that each of the three levels add to $1,000,000 or 100 percent of the organization's budget on the slide. A decomposition tree provides a basis for a manager or analyst to ask questions and make useful comparisons across the organization. For example, is it appropriate for the sales department to have nearly six times the budget of the human resources department?

Show slide 16–8. This is another example of how to use a decomposition tree to organize information for decision-making purposes. The job of a receptionist in a small company has been analyzed and the tree shows how this person's time is spent during the workweek.

This information could be used to help decide such things as what skills are necessary to be hired for this position, which departments should share in the cost of this person, and so forth.

8:50 a.m. Thoughts About Decision Making (5 minutes).

Show slide 16–9, and read the Jonah Lehrer and Malcolm Gladwell quotes and discuss their implications with the class.

8:55 a.m. Break (10 minutes).

9:05 a.m. Scatter Diagrams (10 minutes).

Show slide 16–10. Point out that the schedule allows only a brief overview of scatter diagrams.

Scatter diagrams visually indicate relationships or absence of them between two sets of data. Scatter diagrams compare and show the relationship of one factor to another such as height and weight, work done and people working, day of week and customer traffic, price and sales, accidents and age, and other pairs of factors.

For example, does the speed of a conveyor belt on a production line influence the number of defects produced? Does the amount of fertilizer affect the yield of an acre of corn? Is the income level of a city a true indicator of the potential sales of a product in that city?

Recap: Step-By-Step Instructions to Create a Scatter Diagram

Step 1: Determine which two sets of data need to be compared. Make sure they're appropriately stratified to provide an accurate analysis. For example, if you're comparing productivity of employees to the amount of formal training they've received, it would be best to group new employees and experienced employees separately. Otherwise, you'll not be able to analyze whether the productivity is related to training or to experience on the job.

Step 2: Lay out the vertical and horizontal axes and determine which data to scale along which axis. Certain conventions should be observed. For example, time should be shown horizontally, with earliest times at the left. Although the technique can work with unconventional scaling, it interferes with effectively communicating the information to others. Common sense usually works, but if you want more information, you need to find a reference on graphics presentation.

Step 3: Place a dot or other indication at the intersection of the coordinates that represent each set of data.

Step 4: Examine the resulting pattern of dots for evidence that suggests or denies the existence of relationships in the data. Statistical measures of the degree of actual relationship can be determined using correlation-regression analysis and other techniques.

Resulting Diagrams: Examples

Referring to slide 16–10, explain the different patterns in the scatter diagrams.

A—Positive Relationship. This scatter diagram gives a pretty good indication that when one of the data items goes up, the other probably will too. If you could draw a straight line that went through all points, it would be a perfect relationship (100 percent correlation). That would mean that each move on the vertical axis would have an exactly predictable move along the horizontal axis. For example, if you were buying apples at five cents each, and plotted the number of apples along the vertical axis and the total price paid along the horizontal, it would be a perfectly straight line between the points.

B—Linear, Positive Loose Relationships. This diagram has the basic elements of A, but it's "looser." That means you can't be as sure of the relationship with small changes in one data set. In statistical terms, the correlation is "lower." If you were plotting the height and weight of people, you'd probably get a chart like this. Most people who are 6'4" would weigh more than most who are 4'10". However, you couldn't be sure that someone whose 5'11" weighs more than someone who is 5'9". The looser the relationship, the less you can rely on the data's predictability.

C—Negative Relation. As one piece of data goes up, the other will go down. For example, if you plotted price on the vertical axis and the number sold on the horizontal axis, most products would give a diagram such as this. The higher the price, the fewer sold; the lower the price, the more will sell, other things being equal.

D and E—Non-linear Relationships. Patterns in these diagrams indicate that there probably is some relationship—you can draw a single line that will go fairly near all the points. The line, however, isn't straight. There are statistical formulae to determine the mathematical equation of the line that has the best fit to the dots. This will give you the predicted mathematical relation between the two data sets. Frequently the visual or approximate information you get from the diagram is all that is necessary for decision making.

F—No Relationship. If the scatter diagram looks like this, there is probably no relationship between the data plotted on the vertical (y) axis and the data plotted on the horizontal (x) axis. They are independent of each other. If one goes up, the other may go up, down, or not change. You can make no judgments from data such as this, except that they're probably not related.

9:15 a.m Decision Trees (5 minutes).

Show slide 16–11: Decision Trees. Provide an overview of decision trees. Decision trees help to visualize and follow to conclusion the logic of decisions and their consequences based on events that may result from a decision. As such, a decision tree can provide a basis for either subjective or objective comparison of options. They represent the same data as a multi-level expected-value matrix.

Even if you don't get to the stage of assigning probabilities and calculating specific results, just listing the options and potential results can be helpful in structuring your thinking about the decision.

A graphic "tree" shows the options, providing a map of possible outcomes. When combined with probabilities and expected values, a decision tree presents a quantitative projection of results.

Use slide 16–11 and provide step-by-step instructions for creating a decision tree:

Step 1: Starting at the left of the page, list your decision to be made as the "trunk" of the tree, and the options as the first "limbs."

Step 2: From each of the limbs, divide out into projected results (branches) from a future chance event under different conditions (same set of conditions for each limb). Repeat this step one or two more times, if it is appropriate to consider more than one future chance event.

Step 3: Assign probabilities to the chance events and a dollar value (or other quantifiable value) to the expected implementation cost and resulting profit under those events.

Step 4: Multiply the probabilities and values, and add them up for each initial option. The best option is the one with the most favorable total expected value.

Show slide 16–11 and flesh out the example.

A company must make a decision about purchasing new equipment. The three options under consideration are a permanent tooling investment, a temporary tooling investment, or subcontracting the project. The conditions that may occur in the future, with any of the three options are defined as "success," "partial success," or "failure."

Assign a probability to each of the conditions and a cost and projected profit to each of the options. Let's say that installing permanent tooling will cost $1,000,000, the temporary tooling will cost $400,000, and that subcontracting requires a guarantee of $150,000 to the subcontractor.

Further, suppose that if the new product is a success, the return, if we use permanent tooling, is expected to be $425,000 a year for five years. The return on temporary tooling will be $190,000 per year for three years, and the return from subcontracting will be $80,000 a year for five years.

If the product is a partial success, we'll make 40 percent of the total success figures above. If the product is a failure, we lose our investment plus 10 percent opportunity cost. Now, give the product a 40 percent chance of success and a 30 percent chance of being at least a partial success—which means also that the product has a 30 percent chance of being a failure.

Finally, compute the expected return on each of the three options, given the assumptions we've presented above. To do this, multiply the figures shown beside each branch in the tree above, add them for the three possibilities for each initial choice option, then subtract the required initial investment. This gives you the expected value for each of the options. This is shown following as "Net" figures. The highest numbers generally represent the best choices. The tree on the next slide indicates the best choice to be permanent tooling, given our criteria.

Show slide 16–12. This slide shows the income projections for each of the three options. For the permanent tooling, the weighted average income, using the assumptions discussed before, suggests that a $1 million investment is likely to pay back an additional $775,000 over five years. The temporary tooling and subcontracting options have respective paybacks of $147,000 on a $450,000 investment and $158,000 on a $150,000 investment over five years.

If the company can't get the financing for the $1,000,000 investment, the next best choice is to subcontract, rather than go with temporary tooling. The company can anticipate making a profit in any of the three choices. There is, of course, a 30 percent chance of failure in any of the options.

If we're looking for return-on-investment rather than total profit, the best bet is subcontracting. This is most likely to give us the highest return on the amount invested, but it doesn't give us the highest total profit.

All of this depends on the accuracy of our estimates of cost and probability of success. Good data on those items is important. The actual possible outcomes under the conditions described above would range from a profit of $1,125,000 to a loss of $1,100,000.

Are any of these numbers exactly right? Probably not. This tool just forces the decision maker to structure the costs and possible outcomes into a logical pattern.

9:20 a.m. Other Tools (5 minutes).

Show slide 16–13. Mention a few other tools that can be used to help decision making. Say that economic order quantity and break-even analysis are common tools, which many of your participants might already know, depending on their background. Queuing analysis and linear programming are among the other tools sometimes used to prepare for important corporate decisions.

Note: Economic order quantity (EOQ) and break-even analysis are tools that many of your participants may already know, depending on their school and job experience. However, if you would prefer to teach those tools instead of the expected-value matrices or the other tools presented in module 8, feel free to create the slides and materials to substitute. You can find information on these subjects in any basic management or supervision textbook. The Rue and Byars text in the "For Further Reading" section at the end of this book would be a good source.

9:25 a.m. Apply the Tools to Help You Make a Decision (30 minutes).

Show slide 16–14. Distribute Worksheets 16–1 and 16–4. Also, if you choose, distribute optional Worksheets 16–2 and 16–3.

Announce to the participants that they are to "Use the worksheets to help you make one of the decisions you listed on the pretest during module 1."

The worksheets ask you to apply at least two tools we've worked on in class. Choose the tools that best apply to evaluate options for your decision. For example, you may create a decision matrix, an expected value matrix, a decomposition tree, scatter diagram, or a decision tree to aid your decision.

- ◆ Worksheet 16–1 is a template for a decision matrix.

- ◆ Worksheet 16–2 (optional) provides instruction for using decomposition tree, decision trees, and scatter diagrams. This worksheet is optional, but it has been developed to give the participants a more detailed summary of these tools so they can take it with them. Decide how useful this will be to the participants based on their level of understanding during the training and how likely they are to use the tools described on the worksheet.

- ◆ Worksheet 16–3 (optional) is a template for an expected-value matrix.

- ◆ Worksheet 16–4 asks participants to use the tools covered in this module to help with decision(s) they identified in the pre test taken in module 1. If participants are unable to complete this assignment during the remaining time, suggest that they complete it on their own and bring it back to the following session.

9:55 a.m. Module 8 Summary (5 minutes).

Show slide 16–15 and review the objectives of the modules.

LEARNING CHECK QUESTIONS

You can use the learning check questions and answers in oral or printed form.

Discussion Questions

- ◆ Which of the decision-making tools in this module require groups, and which tools can be done by individuals?

    Answer: All of the tools can be done by individuals, although the data necessary might be better collected by a group.

◆ When should you use a weighted decision matrix?

Answer: When the criteria are not equally important to the decision.

◆ How is an expected value matrix different from a weighted decision matrix?

Answer: The expected value matrix uses real numbers in it, not just index numbers.

◆ Can you create a decision tree with more than three initial branches?

Answer: Yes; you can have as many as necessary.

◆ Is it ever possible to earn exactly the expected value projected from a decision tree?

Answer: Probably not. Expected values are a constructed number that is tied to probability over multiple occurrences.

◆ What would you expect a scatter diagram to look like if you were to chart age (birth to death) against personal income?

Answer: It would probably look like a bell-shaped curve with the center skewed to the right so the highest point would be toward the end of the working years.

10:00 a.m. Thank You for Your Attention.

Show slide 16–16. Edit the slide to include information relevant to your participants.

Worksheet 16–1
Decision Matrix Worksheet

Restate the decision issue that you've been working on here:

_____.

Use the following form to create a decision matrix of possible options and criteria related to the decision you are working with.

Options →					
Criteria ↓ Weight ↓					
Total Points					

Other considerations:

_____

Worksheet 16–2
Decomposition Trees, Decision Trees, and Scatter Diagrams

Other decision analysis tools covered in this unit include decomposition trees, decision trees, and scatter diagrams. Also mentioned, although not covered, are break-even analysis, economic order quantity, queuing analysis, and others. These are too problem-unique to create a template to be filled in and probably would take too long to do during a training session. This sheet explains the process to create three tools so you can try them out on your own, if you wish.

Decomposition Trees Overview

Decomposition trees are a visual aid to understanding the parts that make up a whole. The trees essentially look like traditional organization charts. Their purpose is to help in the "decomposition" or breaking up of a larger item into its components. They could be used for a variety of decision-making or problem-solving needs such as to analyze a budget, review staffing in an organization, or help with a job analysis by a human resources specialist to determine what tasks an individual performs in a job. The results might also be used in the development of a Pareto analysis.

Results or Data Output:

The output is a visual "tree" with relative values indicated for each part.

Step-by-Step Instructions:

Step 1: On the top line of a sheet of paper, list the unit to be analyzed (the entire budget, organization, job, and so forth).

Step 2: Break the whole out into its major parts, and indicate the appropriate value for each part beside it on the next lower line. The value might be in percentages or in real numbers. If percentages, they should add to 100 percent. If real numbers, they should add to the same totals on each line.

Step 3: Continue repeating this process until you have reached the level necessary for whatever analysis you are conducting. Note that each level adds to $1,000,000 or 100 percent.

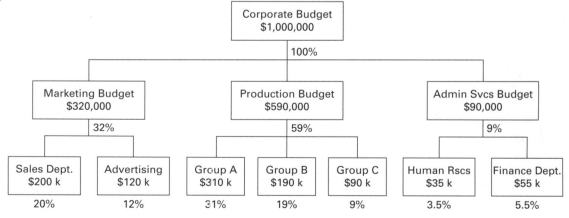

continued on next page

Worksheet 16–2, continued

Decomposition Trees, Decision Trees, and Scatter Diagrams

Decision Trees Overview

Decision trees help to visualize and follow to conclusion the logic of decisions and their consequences based on chance events subsequent to the decision. As such, they provide a basis for either subjective or objective comparison of options. They essentially represent the same data as a multilevel expected-value matrix.

Even if you don't get to the stage of making computations and assigning probabilities, just listing the options and potential results can be helpful in structuring your thinking about the decision.

Knowledge or Input Required: Options available for the decision and the likelihood and value of subsequent events.

Results or Data Output Provided: A graphic "tree" shows the options, providing a map to all projected possible outcomes. When combined with probabilities or expected values, a quantitative projection of results is possible.

Step-by-Step Instructions:

Step 1: Starting at the left of the page, list your decision to be made as the "trunk" of the tree, and the options as the first "limbs."

Step 2: From each of the limbs, divide out into projected results (branches) from a future chance event under different conditions (same set of conditions for each limb). Repeat this step one or two more times, if appropriate to consider more than one future chance event.

Step 3: Assign probabilities to the chance events and a dollar value (or other quantifiable value) to the expected implementation cost and resulting profit under those events.

Step 4: Multiply out the probabilities and values, and add them up for each initial option. The best option is the one with the most favorable total expected value.

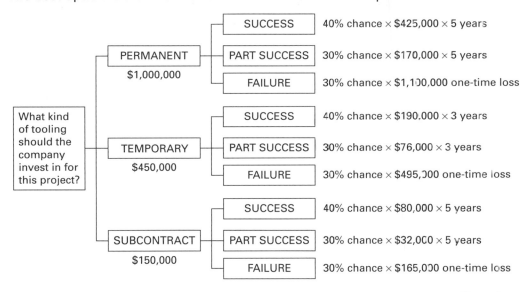

continued on next page

Worksheet 16–2, continued
Decomposition Trees, Decision Trees, and Scatter Diagrams

Scatter Diagram Overview

Scatter diagrams visually indicate relationships or absence of them between two sets of data. Scatter diagrams compare and show the relationship of one factor to another, such as height and weight, price and sales, work done and people working, accidents and age, day of week and customers, and so forth.

Knowledge or Input Required: To use scatter diagrams, the analyst needs information on the sets of data that are to be compared and, in the case of control charts, which standards are required. A basic understanding of the use of graphing is also necessary.

Results or Data Output: Scatter diagrams can suggest whether or not a relationship exists between sets of data. For example, does the speed of a conveyor influence the number of defects produced? Does the amount of fertilizer affect the yield of an acre of corn? Is the income level of a city a true indicator of the potential sales of a product?

Step-by-Step Instructions:

Step 1: Determine which sets of data need to be compared. Make sure they're appropriately stratified to provide an accurate analysis. For example, if you're comparing productivity of employees compared to the amount of formal training they've received, it would be best to group new employees and experienced employees separately. Otherwise, you'll not be able to analyze whether the productivity is related to training or to experience on the job.

Step 2: On graph paper (or by some other appropriate means), lay out vertical and horizontal axes and determine which data to scale along which axis. Certain conventions should be observed. For example, time should be shown horizontally, with earliest times at the left. Although the technique can work with unconventional scaling, it interferes with effectively communicating the information to others. Common sense usually works, but if you want more information, you need to find a reference on graphics presentation.

Step 3: Place a dot or other indication ("x") at the intersection of the coordinates that represent each set of data.

Step 4: Examine the resulting pattern of dots for evidence, which suggests or denies the existence of relationships in the data. Statistical measures of the degree of actual relationship can be determined using correlation-regression analysis and other techniques. (See any book on simple business statistics for further information.)

Worksheet 16–3
Value-Matrix Template

Restate the decision issue that you've been working on here:

_____.

Use the following form to create an expected value matrix of possible options and criteria related to the decision you are working with.

Conditions →					
Options ↓ Weight →					
Expected Value					

Other Considerations

_____

Worksheet 16–4
Reviewing Your Decisions So Far

You have now completed both the creative and analytical portions of making your decision. The remaining two modules will deal with the intangible considerations and developing a final proposal. Before going on to that, collect your worksheets so far and make some notes.

◆ Does the decision matrix you just developed (Worksheet 16–1) look at all like what you expected when you started? (That is, do you have the options and criteria that you anticipated?) If not, what surprises you?

◆ Can you use any of the other analytical techniques described in this module to help with the decision? Which ones, and how? Why would others not work?

◆ Which of the creative techniques from modules 2 through 5 helped you? Are there any others that you now think might have been useful?

◆ Do the seven steps explained in the first module seem to make more sense now?

Discuss your progress toward a final decision and proposal with one of your fellow learners.

MAKING EFFECTIVE DECISIONS

Module 8

Analysis Tools

Slide 16–1

Module 8 Topics

- Describe at least five simple tools that may help improve analysis of information.
  - Decision Matrix, Expected Value, Decomposition Trees, Scatter Diagrams, and Decision Trees
- Apply the appropriate tools to a variety of situations requiring analysis of information.

Slide 16–2

Decision Matrices

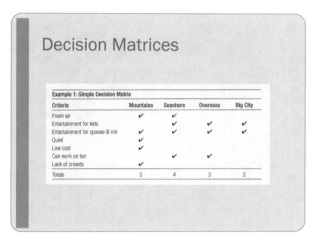

Example 1: Simple Decision Matrix

Criteria	Mountains	Seashore	Overseas	Big City
Fresh air	✔	✔		
Entertainment for kids		✔	✔	✔
Entertainment for spouse & me	✔	✔	✔	✔
Quiet	✔			
Low cost	✔			
Can work on tan		✔	✔	
Lack of crowds	✔			
Totals	5	4	3	2

Slide 16–3

Numerical-Decision Matrices

Example 2: Simple Numerical Decision Matrix
Using a 1–5 scale for each item

Criteria	Mountains	Seashore	Overseas	Big City
Likely Cost	5	3	1	2
Travel Time	2	5	4	3
Relaxation	5	5	2	3
Ease of Travel	5	3	1	2
Family Fun	2	3	5	5
Total Points*	19	19	13	15

*The total points for each column is the sum of the values for each criterion.

Slide 16–4

Weighted Decision Matrix

Example 3: Weighted Decision Matrix
Using a 1–5 scale for each item and a 1–10 scale for the weighting

Criteria	Weight	Mountains	Seashore	Overseas	Big City
Likely cost	9	5 (x9=45)	3 (x9=27)	1 (x9=9)	2 (x9=18)
Travel time	6	2 (x6=12)	5 (x6=30)	4 (x6=24)	3 (x6=18)
Relaxation	4	5 (x4=20)	5 (x4=20)	2 (x4=8)	3 (x4=12)
Ease of travel	4	5 (x4=20)	3 (x4=12)	1 (x4=4)	2 (x4=8)
Family fun	7	2 (x7=14)	3 (x7=21)	5 (x7=35)	5 (x7=35)
Total Points*		111	110	80	91

*The total points for each column are computed by multiplying each criterion value by the weight for that item, then adding.

Slide 16–5

Expected Value Matrices

Unweighted Expected Value Matrix

Policy	Inflation	Depression	Recession	Expected Value	Computed By
Option A	16	11	6	11	(16-11+6)÷3
Option B	8	11	-1	6	(8+11-1)÷3
Option C	4	14	9	9	(4+14+9)÷3

Weighted Expected Value Matrix

Policy	Inflation	Depression	Recession	Expected Value	Computed By
Probability	20%	10%	70%	100%	
Option A	16	11	6	8%	(.2)16+(.1)11+(.7)6
Option B	8	11	-1	2	(.2)8+(.1)11-(.7)1
Option C	4	14	9	8%	(.2)4+(.1)14+(.7)9

Slide 16–6

Decomposition Trees

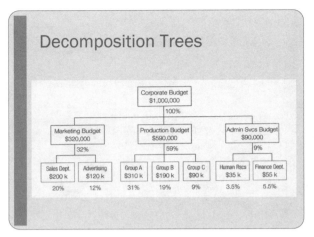

Slide 16–7

Another Decompositon Tree

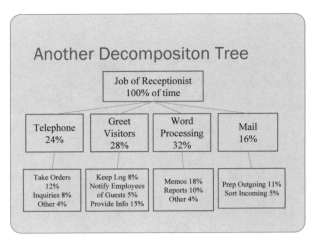

Slide 16–8

Thoughts About Decision Making

- "Absolute confidence is comforting but dangerous."

  —Jonah Lehrer

- "We only really trust conscious decision making."

  —Malcolm Gladwell

Slide 16–9

Scatter Diagrams

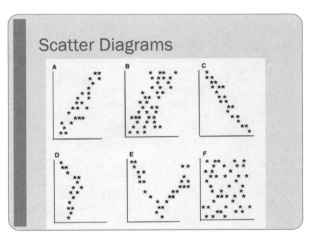

Slide 16–10

Decision Trees

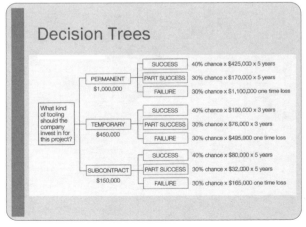

Slide 16–11

Decision Tree Resolution

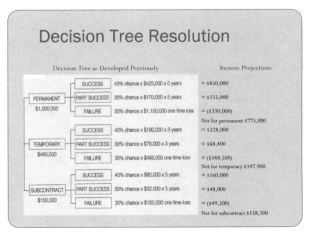

Slide 16–12

Other Tools

- A variety of other statistical and economic models exist that may help an analysis of your decision, including:
  - Economic order quantity
  - Break even analysis
  - Queuing analysis
  - Linear programming

Slide 16–13

Application Exercises

- Use the handouts and one of the decisions you listed on the pretest. Choose at least two tools that might apply to evaluating options for that decision. Create a decision matrix, an expected-value matrix, a decomposition tree, a scatter diagram, or a decision tree to aid your decision.

Slide 16–14

Review

- Describe at least five simple tools that may help improve analysis of information:
  - Decision Matrix, Expected Value, Decomposition Trees, Scatter Diagrams, and Decision Trees
- Apply the appropriate tools to a variety of situations requiring analysis of information.

Slide 16–15

Thank You for Your Attention

- Next meeting:
- Assignment:
- Other announcements?

Slide 16–16

◆

Module 9—The Human Aspect: Emotional and Irrational Factors

Module 9 covers the human aspects of making decisions. This module is a brief summary of a rich and complex subject.

Training Objectives

After completing this module, the participants should be able to

- discuss the merits of group versus individual decision-making processes

- list at least two differences between expert and layperson decision-making requirements

- describe the influence of framing on the decision-making process

- describe the influence of technology on the decision-making process.

Module 9 Time

- Approximately 1.5 hours

Note: This schedule includes time for a quick review at the start and a learning check at the end.

Materials

- Attendance list

- Pencils, pens, and paper for each participant

- Whiteboard or flipchart, and markers

- ◆   Name tags or name tents for each participant

- ◆   Worksheet 17–1: Consider Technology Influences and Human Factors

- ◆   Computer, screen, and projector for displaying PowerPoint slides; alternatively, overhead projector and overhead transparencies

- ◆   PowerPoint slide program (slides 17–1 through 17–13)

- ◆   Software and files

- ◆   This chapter for reference or detailed trainer's notes

- ◆   Optional: music, coffee, or other refreshments.

Module 9 Preparation

Arrive ahead of time to greet the participants and make sure materials are available and laid out for the way you want to run the class.

Sample Agenda

0:00   Welcome the participants.

Have slide 17–1 up on the screen as participants arrive.

Go to slide 17–2 (objectives) as you begin.

Ask for questions and concerns.

0:05   PowerPoint presentation with discussion.

Begin with slide 17–3 and proceed through slide 17–10.

Discuss as necessary. Some discussion questions are on the slides themselves or on notes to the slides.

1:05   Worksheet.

Show slide 17–11 as people work. Distribute Worksheet 17–1: Consider Technology Influences and Human Factors.

1:25   Wrap-up.

Slide 17–12 Review the objectives with the participants.

Ask for questions.

Check for learning (questions can be in oral or written format).

Show slide 17–13 as you dismiss the class. Edit the slide appropriately for your group.

Trainer's Notes

8:00 a.m. Welcome (5 minutes).

Show slide 17–1 as participants arrive.

Take care of housekeeping items.

8:05 a.m. Group Decision Making (35 minutes).

Show slide 17–2 and preview the module objectives.

Show slide 17–3. Tell the participants that predictable things happen as groups make decisions:

- ◆ Groups tend to make decisions more slowly than do individuals.

- ◆ Groups tend to make decisions that are more extreme (exaggerating conservative or radical tendencies) than those made by the individuals.

- ◆ Groups often make weak decisions supported by a minority of the members.

- ◆ Groups may have to compromise, making their decisions less effective than desired.

Managers need to be aware of these concerns. For example, if a quick decision is needed, a group decision should be avoided when possible. Nevertheless, group decision making has real advantages.

Have the participants discuss some recent decisions that they have made or been subject to, and ask whether a group or individual made that decision. Get them thinking about the ideas that will be presented in slides 17–5 and 17–6.

Show slide 17–4.

Read the George Will quote and discuss it briefly with the class before showing the next slide. It should elicit a smile.

Show slide 17–5. Use the bullets as discussion topics.

Some situations where a group decision may be better:

◆ Input is needed from different perspectives (for example from sales, finance, and production).

◆ Support for the decision needs to be developed (members of the team can take more detail and credibility back to their constituencies).

◆ Individuals need to feel involved.

◆ Creativity would be helpful (a wide range of alternatives is needed).

◆ Limited precedents exist for the problem or the decision needed.

◆ A variety of options would be acceptable to management.

Show slide 17–6. Use the bullets as discussion topics.

Group decisions may be undesirable in some situations:

◆ Time is a critical factor.

◆ The group does not have expertise in the issue. (It would become a case of the blind leading the blind.)

◆ The group's norms don't agree with management objectives in the organization.

◆ The group is significantly dominated by one or a few members.

Note that the hazards of group decision making noted earlier on slide 17–3 also are a factor. (Back up and reshow the slide, if it will help make your point.)

Continue the discussion by saying that certain types of decisions are very seldom delegated to a group. Groups don't do well in matters of resolving conflicts, discipline (except as a jury), counseling, motivational problems, and so on. In most organizations, certain tasks are made the sole responsibility of specific managers, and therefore can't be delegated to a group. The group may, however, act as an advisory body or sounding board in the decision-making process by the manager.

If you were to take an organizational behavior class, you'd probably spend at least a third of the course time covering the information summarized in the "Group Dynamics" heading, which includes the emotional aspects at play when groups meet to make a decision. This module is a superficial summary of a dense subject, but is included because the emotional aspects of group decision making are relevant to the subject of decision making in organizations.

8:40 a.m. Experts Versus Laypeople (10 minutes).

Show slide 17–7. Module 1 discusses individuals who are experts in their fields and may have developed sufficient background or experience and innate knowledge to make quick and accurate decisions. Thinking too much about a decision, however, can interfere with the ability to solve insight problems. Surprisingly, scientific research shows, for example, that doctors can often make better diagnoses if they know *less* about the patient.

Ask a food critic about a dish, and—unless you are a food expert yourself— you'll be amazed by his or her analysis. That doesn't mean that a layperson's opinion is "wrong," only that it may be ungrounded, shallow, or difficult to explain.

Gut feeling is powerful and should be acknowledged. Again, lots of research is coming out in books such as *Blink* and *How We Decide*. The scientific research tells us that "gut feelings" should be trusted. The information that has been shared so far in this training program suggests that careful and rational analysis is important in making difficult decisions. Although that is often true, it should not be used to the exclusion of intuition.

Show slide 17–8.

Review the Gary Klein quote with the class and discuss. The point is that experts actually have such a body of knowledge that their intuition is much better than the layperson's. So where someone who is not an expert in a subject might need lots of research before deciding, an expert would not. Therefore, how much individuals should rely on research and how much they can rely on instinct is mostly determined by their existing background in the subject. That's certainly not to say that experts can't be wrong or laypeople can't have excellent insight and instincts.

8:50 a.m. Framing the Decision (10 minutes).

Show slide 17–9. Tell the class something like this: A person's perspective can be altered in amazing ways by how the decision issue is stated. Some of the early work on the concept of framing was done by the psychologists Daniel Kahneman and Amos Tversky in 1974.

They found that the way a problem is stated may significantly alter the level of risk that we assign to a situation. In oversimplified terms, this is the "glass half-full" or "glass half-empty" phenomenon. Both terms accurately describe a 50 percent filled beverage container, but the difference in wording shows that different people look at the same problem differently.

Kahneman and Tversky used college students as subjects in various risk-taking exercises. As just one example, they found a substantial difference between groups in the number of students who said they would buy insurance if they were told there was an 80 percent chance that they *would not* be in an accident than if they were told there was a 20 percent chance that they *would* be in an accident. Obviously, the risk is the same, but simply stated from either a positive or negative perspective. The group that was given the negative perspective (20 percent chance you will be in an accident) was much more likely to purchase insurance.

As you can imagine, this is a popular study in the marketing field. It deserves some significant attention in decision making and problem solving, as well. Ask the learners why this would be true. What are the implications for a salesperson regarding this research? Discuss with the group.

9:00 a.m. Technology Influences (5 minutes).

Show slide 17–10. We see the influence of changing technology every day. And rapid advances in technology bring us more decisions to make. They also make more information available and give us more tools to help make decisions. Nevertheless, more technology is not always a good thing.

One obvious influence of technology on decision making is the availability of tools such as artificial intelligence, computer software, and so forth. Even if the tools are available, the expertise to use them is also needed.

The faster technology changes, the more decisions will be needed and the more pressure comes with the decisions. So high-technology organizations and their managers and teams will experience higher levels of stress. There will also be more need for research to develop new options (because current procedures are made obsolete by new technology). We feel the need to make decisions quickly, often with great levels of risk.

New technology usually makes more data available and increases the risk of information overload. One may find people dreaming of the good old days when chocolate and vanilla were the only choices. That's not likely to happen again, as pointed out by Barry Schwartz in his book, *The Paradox of Choice*. *Note:* You can find some excellent discussion examples there. See the listing in the "For Further Reading" section at the end of this book.

What this all means is that high-technology organizations must become more familiar with the effective decision-making concepts if they are to maintain their competitiveness. Decision making and problem solving must be stream-lined in the process, handled at the most efficient level of the organization, and leveraged with appropriate tools.

9:05 a.m. Application Exercise (20 minutes).

Show slide 17–11. Distribute Worksheet 17–1: Consider Technology Influ-ences and Human Factors. This worksheet continues the pattern of having the participants work on one of the decisions they identified during the module 1 pretest. Individually or in groups, have the participants answer the questions expressed on the worksheet. Move among them to keep them on track and answer any questions.

Ask participants to complete Worksheet 17–1. If you wish, you may also have participants discuss what technology influences exist in their organizations.

9:25 a.m. Module 9 Summary (5 minutes).

Show slide 17–12 and review the objectives of the modules.

LEARNING CHECK QUESTIONS

You can use the learning check questions and answers in oral or printed form.

Discussion Questions

◆   What are some of the influences of technology on decision making?

   Answers: access to databases, speed with which decisions are needed, frequency of changes in procedures, level in the organization at which decisions are made, and so forth.

◆   List some of the advantages of using group decision making.

   Answer: Two heads are better than one; multiple perspectives and more creativity; acceptance of the decision; and so forth.

◆   What types of decisions should *not* be made by a group?

   Answer: Decisions reserved for the manager (because of his or her position within the company), decisions dealing with discipline, decisions that require confidentiality, decisions in which there is no group expertise, and so forth.

◆ What is the concept of framing, and why can you make better decisions if you understand it?

Answer: Framing can be compared to the glass half-full and glass half-empty idea. It's a matter of how you look at a problem or how it's put into context. You'll get better decisions because you are able to see the issue from more than one perspective. Negative framing is more compelling than positive framing.

Multiple Choice Questions

1. Which of the following would be a good reason to use a group to make a decision?

   a. There's a crisis going on, and we need a decision NOW!

   b. The CEO has a strong opinion on the question.

   c. A number of cross-functional issues exist. (*answer*)

   d. The decision group has only one person with expertise in the topic.

2. The term *framing*, as used in supervisory communications, means to

   a. put a matter into a box

   b. put it into a context or perspective (*answer*)

   c. create an illusion of responsibility

   d. reduce the risk and uncertainty

3. When using group decision making, the supervisor should

   a. reserve the right to modify or reject the group's decisions

   b. set certain limitations on the decision before turning it over to the group

   c. have the group assist in generation and evaluation of alternatives but not in the final decision

   d. all of the above (*answer; there's room for argument on this—it depends on the nature of the decision and organizational culture.*)

9:30 a.m. Thank You for Your Attention.

Show slide 17–13. Edit the slide to include information relevant to participants.

Worksheet 17–1

Consider Technology Influences and Human Factors

State the decision you are working with for this training (named by you in the pretest)

_____

What, if any, technological influences affect this decision?

_____

_____

Should this decision be made by a group? Why or why not?

_____

_____

With whom do you need to discuss this decision?

_____

_____

What could affect the timing of this decision? (Deadlines, budgets, cyclical work flows, personalities, and so on)

_____

_____

What other issues facing this decision might be influenced by how the decision is framed?

_____

_____

State the decision in a way someone opposed to your point of view might see it.

_____

_____

MAKING EFFECTIVE DECISIONS

Module 9
The Human Aspect:
Emotional and Irrational Factors

Slide 17–1

Module 9 Topics

- Discuss the merits of group versus individual decision-making processes.
- List at least two differences between expert and layman decision-making requirements.
- Describe the influence of framing on the decision-making process.
- Describe the influence of technology on the decision-making process.

Slide 17–2

Group Decision Making

Some predictable things happen as groups begin to make decisions: They ...

- make decisions more slowly than individuals.
- make decisions that are more extreme than those made by individual members.
- are often subject to weak decisions supported by a minority of the members.
- may have to compromise, making their decisions less effective than desired.

Slide 17–3

Thoughts About Decision Making

- "Football combines the two worst elements of American society: violence and committee meetings."

  —George Will

Slide 17–4

Group Decisions
May Be Better When ...

- Input is needed from different perspectives.
- Support for the decision needs to be developed.
- Individuals need to feel involved.
- Creativity would be helpful.
- Limited precedents exist.
- Any of a variety of options would be acceptable to management.

Slide 17–5

Individual Decisions
May Be Better When ...

- Time is a critical factor.
- The group does not have expertise in the issue.
- Group norms don't agree with management objectives in the organization.
- The group is significantly dominated by one or a few members.

  And for other reasons suggested by the hazards mentioned previously.

Slide 17–6

Experts vs. Laypersons

- Experts have a much more intuitive process.
- Experts have developed complex rating systems that laypeople seldom understand.
- Laypeople may make good decisions but may not be able to explain and document them.
- Our brains (experts and laypeople) detect subtle patterns earlier than we know.

Slide 17–7

Thoughts About Decision Making

- "When experts make decisions, they don't systematically and logically compare all options. … it is much too slow… they size up the situation and act."

  —Gary Klein, *Sources of Power*

  (Experts: nurses, firemen, doctors, etc.)

Slide 17–8

Framing the Decision

- "Framing" is the perspective from which you view the decision. The "cliché" is the glass half full / glass half empty comparison.
- The perspective can make an amazing difference in our decisions.

Slide 17–9

Technology Influences

Slide 17–10

Application Exercise

- Complete the exercise and discuss with your classmates.

Slide 17–11

Review

- Discuss the merits of group versus individual decision-making processes.
- List at least two differences between expert and layman decision-making requirements.
- Describe the influence of framing on the decision-making process.
- Describe the influence of technology on the decision-making process.

Slide 17–12

Thank You for Your Attention

- Next meeting:
- Assignment:
- Other announcements?

Slide 17–13

Module 10—Implementing the Decision: Wrap-Up

Module 10 describes a process for developing a proposal to help get agreement to implement a decision. It should be used with the multiple-day program schedules. It also includes the end-of-program review and posttest material.

Training Objectives

After completing this module, the participants should be able to

- list the important factors to consider in planning to implement a decision

- develop a plan for implementing a decision you have made.

Module 10 Time

- Approximately 2 hours

Note: This schedule includes time for a quick review at the start and a learning check at the end. A 10-minute break is included. Because this is the final module, it also includes time for a posttest and program evaluation.

Materials

- Attendance list

- Pencils, pens, and paper for all participants

- Whiteboard or flipchart, and markers

- Name tags or name tents for all participants

- Worksheet 18–1: Finalizing Your Proposal

- Evaluation Instrument 18–1: Posttest on Decision Making

◆   Computer, screen, and projector for displaying PowerPoint slides; alternatively, overhead projector and overhead transparencies

◆   PowerPoint slide program (slides 18–1 through 18–14)

◆   Software and files

◆   This chapter for reference or detailed trainer's notes

◆   Certificates of completion for all participants

◆   Evaluation Instrument 5–2: Final Full-Program Evaluation Form

◆   Optional: music, coffee, or other refreshments.

Module Preparation

Arrive ahead of time to greet the participants and make sure materials are available and laid out for the way you want to run the class. Turn on and test computer equipment.

Sample Agenda

0:00   Welcome the participants.

Have slide 18–1 up on the screen as people arrive.

Go to slide 18–2 as you introduce the objectives.

Ask for questions and concerns.

0:05   PowerPoint with discussion.

Begin with slide 18–3, and proceed through slide 18–6. These slides have more content and notes than those in previous modules.

0:45   Break.

0:55   Worksheet.

Show slide 18–7 as participants complete Worksheet 18–1: Finalizing Your Proposal.

1:30   Wrap-up.

Check for learning; see questions below.

Review the entire program—slides 18–8 and 18–9

Show slide 18–10. Discuss the Lehrer quote with the class.

Show slide 18–11. Hand out Evaluation Instrument 18–1. As participants work on the test, hand out Evaluation Instrument 5–2: Final Full-Program Evaluation Form.

1:50   Show answers to posttest on slide 18–12. Discuss as necessary.

Show slide 18–13 and discuss as desired.

2:00   Show slide 18–14: Farewell. Edit slide to include any pertinent information.

Trainer's Notes

8:00 a.m. Welcome (5 minutes).

Show slide 18–1 as participants arrive.

Take care of housekeeping items.

8:05 a.m. Winning Proposals (40 minutes).

Show slide 18–2, and preview the module objectives.

Show slide 18–3.

Below are points to cover about creating a proposal to implement a decision.

The level of formality of proposals varies greatly. Your proposal may take the form of a feasibility report, a specific form to turn in to your company's suggestion system, an informal chat with the boss, or any number of other written or oral formats. The issues you are addressing and the level of familiarity of your boss (or other decision makers) with those issues will influence how you approach and develop the proposal.

Some of your first steps would be as follows:

Classify your audience. Begin the design of a proposal by classifying the audience that will be evaluating the recommendations. Are they "expert," "technician," "executive," "layperson," or a "combined" audience?

Remind the learners of the characteristics of these audiences as covered in module 1. Creating your proposal with the readers in mind allows them to easily pick out information of interest.

Establish credibility. This step is sometimes unnecessary or even impossible. If you (or your group) are well-known to the decision makers, you are probably stuck with your existing reputation—at least in the short run. If that reputation is good, be sure to keep it that way. If your reputation is not good (or you are unknown to the decision makers), you may want to use additional sources to support your idea. In any case, to gain or maintain credibility, you need to carefully present and document your recommendations.

Credibility is, of course, in the eye of the beholder. It always pays to scope out your audience and play to your strengths and their preferences as you design your proposal. Sometimes you can be more credible if you remind the decision maker of your credentials or results you've achieved in the past. Sometimes showing that the idea has worked elsewhere in similar circumstances (maybe for a competitor) will establish that it might be worth trying.

Whatever process you use, the key point is to maneuver the people who must accept and implement the decision into a willingness to read about or listen to the idea. They have to believe that you may have something worthwhile to say.

Ensure a focus on your idea. It has to be possible for the decision makers to get *to* the idea. Don't allow a sloppy presentation, with misspelled words or mistakes, to take away from your great ideas. But, looks aren't everything: An exquisitely produced, superbly printed, and graphically memorable proposal that is shallow or unworkable will still not sell. Besides, if it's too slick, management will wonder why you spent so much time and money on the presentation instead of doing your job.

The objective of proposal packaging can be summed up by saying that it must be an "appropriate quality" for the situation at hand. Avoid distractions that will inhibit your message. This applies to both written and oral presentations.

Show slide 18–4.

Discuss the Malcolm Gladwell quote with the class.

Show slide 18–5.

Not all 11 categories suggested on this slide and the next are needed in every proposal. Depending on the topic and other circumstances, several of these ideas may be handled in a single sentence, whereas others may require pages or hours of discussion. These topics are presented in a sequence that will work for most proposals, but this order is not sacrosanct. Rearrange the ideas if it seems to make sense for the topic at hand.

1. Begin by expressing the need for a change. State early and clearly *what* the proposal is and *why* it is needed. The only exception to this rule is if the proposal is so radical that stating it up front will result in an immediate rejection of the idea. In that situation, you will need to build up to the recommendation through discussion. Normally, though, that takes too much of the audience's time, so get right to the point. If this takes you more than three sentences, you need to rethink it and focus more carefully.

2. Define the problem or opportunity that led to the proposal. What brought this idea to mind? Remember, management frequently looks at problems or opportunities mainly in terms of numbers. How much did it cost? How much more could be produced? How much time could be saved?

The *"M"* resources might cue you to a way of defining the problem. What *m*oney, *m*aterials, *m*ethods, *m*inutes, *m*achinery, *m*aintenance, *m*anagement, *m*arkets, *m*anpower, *m*ilieux, or *manuscripts* are doing less than they could? (OK—that's a stretch. Look up *milieux*, though, and you'll see why it works.)

3. Understand the background of the problem or opportunity. How did the underlying problem or opportunity develop? Has it always been there, or did some change occur that has caused it?

4. Emphasize the need for a solution. What will happen if no changes are made? Will the organization still be able to operate? This "down-side discussion" needs to be tied to specific dollar and time costs whenever possible.

5. Specify the benefits of adopting the proposal. What specific savings or improvement will occur as a result of implementing the change? Increased production, faster turnaround, reduced complaints, or what else? Once again, tying these to defensible and clear numbers will be helpful for most decision makers. You need to be enthusiastic about the benefits, yet not come across as a "used-car salesman."

Note that the proposal details have still not been divulged. Presenting the benefits (instead of details) at this point is part of developing a momentum. The intent is to get the decision maker into a receptive enough mood to listen to the details. Later in the proposal is the place to specify the details, but first, you need to sell the benefits that will come out of the proposed changes or ideas. "Benefits-first" is a technique taught in nearly every sales class.

Show slide 18–6.

6. Define the nature and scope of the proposal. What change is being proposed, and where will it be implemented? Does it involve one person or one department or a company-wide effort? How pervasive will the effects of the change be? What other areas of the organization will be affected in addition to the areas in which the change occurs? Who else, if anyone, needs to be involved?

7. Present a plan for implementing the decision. What methods will be used in implementation? What tasks have to be done—and by whom? What facilities and equipment will be needed? When do these things need to happen? *Clarity* is the keyword in the implementation plan. Use analogies, examples, simple graphics, and terms and formats comfortable to the audience, and include charts, photographs, and tables.

The implementation plan, however, should include only the key points. Further details can be put in an appendix to a written proposal or in handouts or visuals to be used only if needed during an oral proposal. This style of presentation allows the presenter to engage in an unobstructed overview, yet drop to a deeper level, if necessary. The appropriate level depends on knowing the audience and whether the decision maker will be involved with simple approval/disapproval, or in the actual process of implementation.

8. Provide support for the proposal. Do you personally have any experience relevant to the proposal? Can you cite examples of where it has been tried before? Who else in the organization (or outside) may have the background to help? Are there articles, books, or other reference sources you could cite to support the ideas? Remember to include the names and credentials of people who helped develop the original idea and others in the organization with whom the proposal has already been discussed.

9. Discuss the likelihood of success. No implementation of change is going to come off perfectly. Of course, your proposal should have more going for it than against it, but don't leave yourself open to criticism by ignoring potential problems. It is far better to bring up objections yourself than to respond to them only when challenged by the decision makers. Disarm this possibility by listing criticisms and problems, with either a valid response to each or a summation of the consequences if these problems actually interfere.

10. Explain and justify the cost of the proposal. It is a typical sales technique to leave discussion of the cost until the sale is made. Sooner or later, however, the issue of cost will come up. Be ready to present the costs accurately and in projected cost/benefit (value or return-on-investment) terms. Remember, too, that total cost includes employee-hours, materials, and many other things. In some organizations, the kind of cost may be as important as the amount of the cost. For example, an organization may have a budget for equipment but not for hiring people, or capital expenses rather than operating expenses. These limitations could be due to different tax treatments or legislative mandates for hiring or many other reasons. It may be necessary to specify costs by category for this type of situation. Overall, do as much as possible to focus on the positive value created by the proposed change.

11. Document, if necessary. In most proposals, the documentation can be delivered in an appendix to the proposal.

The term *appendix*, of course, refers to an organ in the body that no one pays any attention to unless something goes wrong. An appendix should include any supporting material that might be of interest to the decision maker, but which is so detailed that it would impede the flow of ideas. Examples might include charts, surveys, computations, input data, flow charts, articles, lists of personnel, and so forth. Similar information needs to be on hand or available for review following an oral presentation. The decision maker should be given the documentation for later review or as a reminder, in order to allow effective consideration of the proposal.

8:45 a.m. Break (10 minutes).

8:55 a.m. Application Exercise (40 minutes).

Show slide 18–7. Distribute Worksheet 18–1: Finalizing Your Proposal and help participants in completing their responses to the questions it poses.

9:35 a.m. Program Summary (10 minutes).

Show slides 18–8 and 18–9. Delete from the program summary any modules not covered in the version of the program you presented to this class. Edit the slides to reflect the modules you presented to this class.

PROGRAM SUMMARY

Slides 18–8 and 18–9 just restate the topics presented in each of the 10 modules. Use whatever review technique you prefer. Have the participants look at their final worksheet for each of the modules as you go over things. The module objectives for each are summarized below.

MODULE 1—THE DECISION-MAKING PROCESS: ANATOMY OF A DECISION

- ◆ List and explain the steps by which a decision is made.

- ◆ Explain the benefits of a structured decision-making process.

- ◆ Determine the relative importance of a decision.

MODULE 2—THE CREATIVE PROCESS: DEVELOPING OPTIONS

- ◆ Explain the importance of creativity in decision making.

- ◆ Clarify the goal of a decision.

- ◆ Develop or identify viable options from which to choose.

- ◆ Calculate the degree of risk related to a decision.

MODULE 3—BARRIERS TO CREATIVITY

- ◆ Identify six kinds of barriers that may affect effective decision making.

- ◆ Identify personal traits related to decision making.

- ◆ Identify group traits related to decision making.

MODULE 4—OVERCOMING BARRIERS TO CREATIVITY

- ◆ Explain four techniques for overcoming barriers to creativity.

- ◆ Develop a personal plan for reducing at least two common barriers.

MODULE 5—TOOLS TO IMPROVE CREATIVITY

- ◆ Describe at least five simple tools that may help improve creativity.

- ◆ Apply the appropriate tools to a variety of situations requiring creativity.

MODULE 6—THE ANALYTIC PROCESS: NARROWING DOWN THE OPTIONS

- ◆ Identify significant sources of data for decision-making analysis.

- ◆ Determine the value of collecting additional information.

- ◆ Explain and use the concept of Pareto analysis.

MODULE 7—USING EVERYDAY STATISTICS

- ◆ Define probability using common examples.

- ◆ Use the concept of probability to explain common simple decision-making situations.

- ◆ Explain the process and uses of sampling data related to decision making.

MODULE 8—USING TOOLS TO IMPROVE ANALYSIS

♦ Describe at least five simple tools that may help improve analysis of information.

♦ Apply the appropriate tools to a variety of situations requiring analysis of information.

MODULE 9—THE HUMAN ASPECT: EMOTIONAL AND IRRATIONAL FACTORS

♦ Discuss the merits of group versus individual decision-making processes.

♦ List at least two differences between expert and layperson decision-making requirements.

♦ Describe the influence of framing on the decision-making process.

♦ Describe the influence of technology on the decision-making process.

MODULE 10—IMPLEMENTING THE DECISION: WRAP-UP

♦ List the important factors to consider in planning to implement a decision.

♦ Develop a plan for implementing a decision you have made.

9:45 a.m. A Final Thought on Decision Making (10 minutes).

Show slide 18–10. Review the Jonah Lehrer quote with the class.

Show slide 18–11. Distribute Evaluation Instrument 18–1: Posttest on Decision Making.

Note: The 20-question true-false test should only require about 5 minutes. When most everyone appears to be finished, move on to slide 18–12 and let individual participants grade themselves, unless you prefer to grade them.

9:55 a.m. Last Thoughts on Decision Making (5 minutes).

Show slide 18–13. Discuss the Malcolm Forbes, Malcolm Gladwell, and Joanne Lee quotes.

LEARNING CHECK QUESTIONS

You can use the learning check questions and answers in oral or printed form.

Discussion Questions

Ask the participants these questions for reflection:

◆ Analyze a recent decision with which you are familiar (ask for a volunteer to answer).

What was the process used in making it?

Was adequate critical thinking used?

Did any organizational structure, climate, or cultural factor have an influence on the decision? Was technology an influence on this decision in any way?

How else could the decision have been framed? Would that have influenced the result?

◆ Name a couple of the hazards of *over*developing a proposal before it is presented.

Answers: Minor changes become more difficult; may be wasted effort if the idea is not accepted.

◆ If the person who will receive and decide on the proposal is an expert in the field, what sort of approach might you want to use? How about if he or she is a layperson?

Answers: For the expert, cite explicit sources of why the idea is good and provide a detailed appendix with facts and figures. *For the layperson,* a more anecdotal approach will work, including stories of why it's needed and where it has worked and what personal benefits can they expect.

◆ Why is it frequently appropriate to delay discussion of details about a proposal until later in the presentation.

Answer: It's important that the big idea gets accepted first.

10:00 a.m. A Final Farewell.

Show slide 18–14. Edit this slide to include the appropriate details. Ask participants to complete and return their evaluation form, Evaluation Instrument 5–2. Each organization will probably have its own policies on this. Typically, attendees are asked to either leave it on the table as they exit, put it in an envelope (provided), or give it to their supervisor or training representative once they return to their job site. Each instructor or organization will have specific policies.

Worksheet 18–1
Finalizing Your Proposal

Complete as much of the following as you can in the time available. Take this with you following the training program, and use it to develop your ideas more fully.

In no more than two sentences, what is your idea?

1	

What format and level of formality is needed?

2	Written, oral, other? Formal report, casual conversation or in-between?

Define the audience that will consider the idea:

3	Who is it? How much do they know?
	The audience is: __Expert __Technician __Executive __Layman __Mixed or unknown

How well developed must the proposal be?

4	Just enough to get the idea accepted, or very complete? Does it need to be divided into planning, then implementation? What quality issues apply in this case?

How can you enhance the proposal's credibility?

5	What in your record (or your team's) can you cite? How can you make it more believable? What politics may be going on regarding this issue? What else can help the audience agree with it?

continued on next page

Worksheet 18–1, continued
Finalizing Your Proposal

What background is needed for the audience?

6	What change (if any) happened to cause this problem or opportunity?
	What are the consequences of not dealing with the proposal being made?

What support exists for the proposal?

7	What specific support do you have for the idea in terms of underutilized resources, excessive costs, poor allocation of people or equipment, customer complaints, employee dissatisfaction, awkward procedures, new market opportunities, issues with facilities, and so on? Cite specific numbers and costs. If you don't know them now, where can you find them before you finalize the proposal? Personal experience? Other people who agree so far? Books or articles? Other places it has worked?

What are the benefits of this idea?

8	List the expected benefits, quantifying them when possible.

What are the specifics: What, who, when, and where?

9	Specifically, what are you asking the decision maker to agree to at this time? Who else will be involved or affected? What other offices, locations, departments, and people will be involved or affected? When should this change happen?

continued on next page

Worksheet 18–1, continued
Finalizing Your Proposal

As much as possible prior to approval, what is the general implementation plan and what actions are needed?

10	Include the schedule, list of tasks, methods, facilities involved, and so on.

Is there a possible downside to the proposal?

11	List any significant issues that might arise, as well as how you would deal with them or the consequences.

What will the proposal cost to implement?

12	What is the budget (by category if necessary), who will pay for it?
	What is the expected ROI (return-on-investment) or cost-benefit ratio?

What materials do you need in the appendix?

13	Charts, surveys, computations, input data, articles, lists of personnel, references, citations, and so on.

Additional Notes:

Evaluation Instrument 18–1

Posttest on Decision Making

Circle either T (true) or F (false):

T   F   1. We all make hundreds of decisions every day.

T   F   2. All decisions are made in an essentially similar pattern.

T   F   3. The first step in decision making is to determine if one is really needed.

T   F   4. Deadlines are an influence on a decision's importance.

T   F   5. Decisions that can be changed later are often less critical.

T   F   6. Technological capability is an example of a limitation in decision making.

T   F   7. Most of us are born with more creativity than we use.

T   F   8. Being stuck in a rut is an example of an emotional block.

T   F   9. We can improve our creativity with practice.

T   F   10. Choices should be evaluated as they appear.

T   F   11. Decision making applies to all phases of management or supervision.

T   F   12. Checklists and catalogs can be idea-generating tools.

T   F   13. Intuition is more important than rational thought in the early stages of decision making.

T   F   14. Limits should be established early in the decision-making process.

T   F   15. Tolerance for risk influences individual decision making.

T   F   16. Listing possible sources of information, then trying to determine which is most important, is a simplified form of Pareto analysis.

T   F   17. A decision matrix can be used to aid almost any decision.

T   F   18. It is better to present ideas to individuals than to groups.

T   F   19. Brainstorming can be done by any individual to help make decisions.

T   F   20. "Framing" the decision properly is helpful but not essential.

continued on next page

Evaluation Instrument 18–1, continued

Posttest on Decision Making

Posttest Answers: 1 T; 2 T; 3 T; 4 F (may be urgent but not important); 5 T; 6 T; 7 T; 8 T; 9 T; 10 F; 11 T; 12 T; 13 T; 14 T (but only limited limits); 15 T; 16 T; 17 T; 18 T (usually); 19 F; 20 F (it is essential).

MAKING EFFECTIVE DECISIONS

Module 10
Implementing the Decision

Slide 18–1

Module 10 Topics

- List the important factors to consider in planning to implement a decision.
- Develop a plan for implementing a decision you have made.
- Review and wrap up.

Slide 18–2

Four Key Points to a Proposal

- Design it to an appropriate level.
- Focus on the audience.
- Make the decision credible.
- Avoid distractions; make the idea central.

Slide 18–3

Thoughts About Decision Making

- We, as human beings, have a "storytelling" problem. We are a bit too quick to come up with explanations for things we don't really have an explanation for.

—Malcolm Gladwell

Slide 18–4

Writing the Proposal

- Why the change is needed
- What led to this need
- Background of the problem or opportunity
- Need for a solution
- Benefits of adopting the proposal

Slide 18–5

Writing the Proposal

- Cover nature and scope of the proposal.
- Plan for implementation.
- Generate support for the proposal.
- Discuss likelihood for success.
- Explain and justify the cost.
- Document, as necessary.

Slide 18–6

Application Exercise

- Use the worksheet to draft a rough copy of the proposal to implement your decision.
- Discuss it briefly with others.

Slide 18–7

Program Summary

- The decision-making process
- The creative process
- The barriers to creativity
- Overcoming those barriers
- Tools to help improve creativity

And, switching from inductive to deductive…

Slide 18–8

Program Summary

- The analytic process: Narrowing down the options
- Everyday uses of simple statistical concepts
- Tools to help improve analysis
- The human aspect: emotional and irrational factors
- Implementing the decision

Slide 18–9

Thoughts About Decision Making

- "Simple problems require reason; complex problems require emotions. Novel problems also require reason. With difficult problems one must allow for uncertainty. You know more than you know."

—Jonah Lehrer

Slide 18–10

Posttest

- Complete the posttest worksheet.
- If you finish before others, complete the program evaluation.
- We'll review the posttest answers next.

Slide 18–11

Final Posttest Answers

1. True
2. True
3. True
4. False (maybe *urgency*, but not *importance*)
5. True
6. True
7. True
8. True
9. True
10. False
11. True
12. True
13. True
14. True (but only *limited* limits)
15. True
16. True
17. True
18. True (usually, at least)
19. False (it's a group tool)
20. False (it *is* essential)

Slide 18–12

Last Thoughts on Decisions

- "It is much more pleasant to make the decision than to justify it."
  - Malcolm Forbes
- "Decisions made quickly can be every bit as good as ones we agonize over."
  - Malcolm Gladwell
- "Life is full of choices… and sometimes all of them are yucky!"
  - Joanne Lee

Slide 18–13

A Final Farewell

- Complete the program evaluation.
- Complete any other paperwork.
- Plan the class reunion (or follow-up).

Slide 18–14

◆

Using the Online Materials

Open the webpage www.ASTD.org/decisionmakingtraining in your web browser.

Content of the Website

The website that accompanies this workbook on decision-making training contains two types of files. All of these files can be used on a variety of computer platforms.

- **Adobe.pdf documents.** These include worksheets and evaluations.

- **PowerPoint slides.** These presentations add interest and depth to many of the training activities included in the workbook.

Computer Requirements

To read or print the .pdf files included on the website, Adobe Acrobat Reader software must be installed on your system. This program can be downloaded free of cost from the Adobe website, www.adobe.com.

To use or adapt the contents of the PowerPoint presentation files on the website, Microsoft PowerPoint software must be installed on your system. If you just want to view the PowerPoint documents, you must have an appropriate viewer installed on your system. Microsoft provides downloads of various viewers free of charge on its website, www.microsoft.com.

Printing From the Website

TEXT FILES

You can print the training materials using Adobe Acrobat Reader. Just open the .pdf file and print as many copies as you need. The following .pdf documents can be printed directly from the website:

- Worksheet 2–1. Decision Making: Needs Analysis

- Worksheet 3–1. Preplanning for Training Program

- Worksheet 9–1. Icebreaker

- Worksheet 9–2. Decision Analysis Sheet

- Worksheet 10–1. Decision Analysis Sheet

- Worksheet 11–1. Creativity Barriers

- Worksheet 11–2. Word Puzzles

- Worksheet 12–1. Overcoming Creativity Barriers

- Worksheet 12–2. Creativity Stimulators

- Worksheet 13–1. Brainstorming Techniques

- Worksheet 13–2. Checklists and Catalogs

- Worksheet 13–3. Attribute Listing

- Worksheet 13–4. Cause-Effect Fishbone Diagrams

- Worksheet 13–5. Cause-Effect Matrix Diagrams

- Worksheet 13–6. Morphological Analysis

- Worksheet 13–7. Decision-Making Worksheet for Module 5

- Worksheet 14–1. Sources of Information

- Worksheet 15–1. Probability, Combinations, and Permutations

- Worksheet 15–2. Statistical Techniques

- Worksheet 16–1. Decision Matrix Worksheet

- Worksheet 16–2. Instructions for Using Decomposition Trees, Decision Trees, and Scatter Diagrams

- Worksheet 16–3. Value-Matrix Template

- Worksheet 16–4. Reviewing Your Decisions So Far

- Worksheet 17–1. Consider Technology Influences and Human Factors

- Worksheet 18–1. Finalizing Your Proposal

- Evaluation Instrument 5–1. Level 1 Evaluation Form

- Evaluation Instrument 5–2. Final Full-Program Evaluation Form

- Evaluation Instrument 9–1. Pretest on Decision Making

- Evaluation Instrument 18–1. Posttest on Decision Making

POWERPOINT SLIDES

The PowerPoint presentation slides required for the decision-making training program or the topic-specific modules in chapters 9 through 18 are located on the website as .ppt files. You can access individual slides by opening the PowerPoint presentations for the specific module of interest. Just open the .ppt files and print as many copies as you need. You can also make handouts of the presentations by printing threes "slides" per page.

Adapting the PowerPoint Slides

You may find it useful to modify or otherwise customize the slides by opening and editing them in the appropriate application. You must, however, retain the denotation of the original source of the material; it is illegal to pass it off as your own work. You may indicate that a document was adapted from this workbook, written by Robert Vaughn, and copyrighted by ASTD. The files will open as "Read Only," so before you adapt them, save them onto your hard drive under a different filename.

Showing the PowerPoint Slides

The following PowerPoint presentations are included on the website:

- *Module 1 The Decision-Making Process.ppt*

- *Module 2 The Creative Process.ppt*

- *Module 3 Barriers to Creativity.ppt*

- *Module 4 Overcoming Barriers to Creativity.ppt*

- *Module 5 Tools to Improve Creativity.ppt*

- *Module 6 The Analytic Process.ppt*

- *Module 7 Using Everyday Statistics.ppt*

- *Module 8 Using Tools to Improve Analysis.ppt*

- *Module 9 The Human Aspect.ppt*

- *Module 10 Implementing the Decision.ppt*

The presentations are in .ppt format, which means that they will automatically show full screen when you double click on the filename. You can also open Microsoft PowerPoint and launch them from there.

Use the space bar, enter key, or mouse clicks to advance through a presentation. Press the backspace key to back up. Use the escape key to exit a presentation. If you want to blank the screen to black as the group discusses a point, press the B key. Press it again to restore the show. If you want to blank the screen to a white background, do the same with the W key. Table A-1 summarizes these instructions.

Table A-1 Navigating Through a PowerPoint Presentation

KEY	POWERPOINT "SHOW" ACTION
Space bar *or* Enter *or* Mouse click	Advance through custom animations embedded in the presentation.
Backspace	Back up to the last projected element of the presentation.
Escape	Abort the presentation.
B *or* b B *or* b *(repeat)*	Blank the screen to black. Resume the presentation.
W *or* w W *or* w *(repeat)*	Blank the screen to white. Resume the presentation.

Practice with the slides before you use them to conduct a workshop. You should be able to expand on the content confidently; this workbook will provide additional support and information for you. If you want to engage your training participants fully (rather than worry about how to show the next slide), become familiar with this simple technology before you need to use it. A good practice is to insert notes into the Speaker's Notes feature of the PowerPoint program, print them out, and have them in front of you when you present the slides.

Adams, James L. *Conceptual Blockbusting: A Guide to Better Ideas* (4th edition). New York: Basic Books, 2001.

Bazerman, Max H. *Judgment in Managerial Decision Making* (3rd edition). New York: John Wiley, 1994.

Beach, Lee R. *Making the Right Decision: Organizational Culture, Vision and Planning.* Prentice-Hall. Englewood Cliffs, NJ: Prentice-Hall, 1993.

Beich, Elaine, editor. *ASTD Handbook for Workplace Learning Professionals.* Alexandria, VA: ASTD Press, 2008.

Evans, James R. *Creative Thinking in the Decision and Management Sciences.* Cincinnati: South Western, 1991.

Gladwell, Malcolm. *Blink: The Power of Thinking Without Thinking.* New York: Little, Brown, 2005.

Holman, Peggy, and Tom Devane, editors. *The Change Handbook: Group Methods for Changing the Future.* San Francisco: Berrett-Koehler, 1999.

Houp, Kenneth W., Thomas E. Pearsall, Elizabeth Tebeaux, and Sam Dragga. *Reporting Technical Information,* 11th ed. New York: Oxford University Press, 2005.

Kahneman, Daniel, and Amos Tversky. "Prospect Theory: An Analysis of Decision Under Risk." *Econometrica* 47 (March 1979) pp. 263–291.

Kepner, Charles H., and Benjamin B. Tregoe. *The Rational Manager: A Systematic Approach to Problem Solving and Decision Making.* Princeton, NJ: Kepner-Tregoe, 1965.

Kirkpatrick, Donald L. *Evaluating Training Programs* (2nd edition). San Francisco: Berrett-Koehler, 2004.

Kirkpatrick, Donald L. "Great Ideas Revisited: Revisiting Kirkpatrick's Four-Level Model." *Training and Development Journal* 50 (1) (1996), pp. 54–57.

Lehrer, Jonah. *How We Decide.* New York: Houghton Mifflin, 2009.

McCall, Morgan M. Jr., and Robert F. Kaplan. *Whatever It Takes: The Realities of Managerial Decision Making* (2nd edition). Englewood Cliffs, NJ: Prentice-Hall 1990.

Noe, Raymond A. *Employee Training and Development* (2nd edition). New York: McGraw-Hill, 2002.

Nutt, Paul C. *Why Decisions Fail—Avoiding the Blunders and Traps That Lead to Debacles.* San Francisco: Berrett-Koehler, 2002.

Phillips, Jack. *Handbook of Training Evaluation and Measurement Methods* (3rd edition). Houston: Gulf Publishing, 1998.

Rue, Leslie W., and Lloyd L. Byars. *Supervision: Key Link to Productivity.* New York: McGraw-Hill–Irwin, 2003.

Schwartz, Barry. *The Paradox of Choice: Why More Is Less,* Harper Perennial. New York: Harper Perennial, 2004.

Stolovitch, Harold D., and Erica J. Keeps. *Telling Ain't Training.* (Alexandria, VA: ASTD Press, 2002).

Vaughn, Robert H. *Decision Making and Problem Solving in Management: Tools and Techniques for Managers and Teams* (3rd edition). Cleveland: Crown Custom Publishing, 2007.

Vaughn, Robert H. *The Professional Trainer: A Comprehensive Guide to Planning, Delivering and Evaluating Training Programs* (2nd edition). San Francisco: Berrett-Koehler, 2005.

◆

Robert H. Vaughn, Ph.D., is president of Arvon Management Services, located near Cleveland, Ohio. He currently works as an author, speaker, and business consultant. Bob is the former Dean of Business and a Professor Emeritus of Management at Lakeland Community College in Ohio. His background includes management and staff positions in the fields of publishing, training, banking, industrial engineering, human resources planning, the military, and higher education. Bob holds undergraduate degrees in industrial management and journalism, an MBA in organizational behavior and

Photo by Eric Vaughn Photography: **www.ericvaughnphotography.com**.

organizational development, and a PhD in business administration, and he has additional postgraduate coursework in adult education. He has had articles published in a variety of professional journals and been a speaker at several regional and national conferences. Bob is also the author of **The Professional Trainer: A Comprehensive Guide to Planning, Delivering and Evaluating Training Programs**, published by Berrett-Koehler, and **Decision Making and Problem Solving in Management: Tools and Techniques for Managers and Teams**, published by Crown Custom Publishing. You can contact Bob with comments or suggestions through his website: **www.ArvonManagement.com**.

◆